Our Life After Death or the Teaching of the Bible Concerning the Unseen World

Reverend Arthur Chambers

Our Life After Death

OR

The Teaching of the Bible Concerning the Unseen World

BY THE

REVEREND ARTHUR CHAMBERS

ASSOCIATE OF KING'S COLLEGE, LONDON
VICAR OF BROCKENHURST, HAMPSHIRE, ENGLAND

PHILADELPHIA
GEORGE W. JACOBS & CO.
PUBLISHERS

PREFACE

ONE or two remarks may not be without interest to my brothers and sisters in America, into whose hands this authorized edition of my little book— "Our Life after Death"—may fall.

When, in the early part of 1894, I published this work in the city of London, I little expected that it would find its way into so many thousands of Christian homes in this and other lands.

Nor did I anticipate that there was in store for me the happiness of learning that hundreds of sorrowing and anxious ones had found in its pages light, comfort, and hope.

But so it has been. In England, the book has now reached its forty-seventh edition, at Leipzig a German issue has lately appeared, to America several thousand copies have been sent from London, and,—better still—more than twelve hundred letters have reached me from all quarters of the world, to tell me that my words have enabled the writers to

see a glorious sunshine behind the gloomy clouds
of bereavement and death.

From the depths of my heart I thank God for
using me as an humble instrument in clearing away
a little of the mist of indefinite thought that has
gathered around, and obscured, His revealed truth
as concerns "the Life of the World to come."

The book was not the outcome of a few weeks,
or months of thought. For many years before it
was written, an ever-growing conviction was forcing itself upon my mind that the current ideas concerning our Hereafter were very vague and unsatisfactory.

I could not help noticing that, although preachers
and writers acknowledged the fact of a World Beyond, they seemed, on the whole, to have no *definite* idea on the subject. Man himself after death,
as well as the World into which he then enters,
alike appeared lost in a murky atmosphere of ab-
straction.

Sometimes I conversed with earnest students of
the Bible—men much older and more experienced
than myself—who did not hesitate to frankly tell

me that the whole question of man's future was veiled in impenetrable mystery ; that the border-line must be crossed before any of the secrets could be known. This troubled me and depressed me.

I could not help thinking that earnest men and women were not wrong in wanting to know something of that World to which they are told they will go.

I felt, moreover, that if the Gospel of Jesus Christ had "brought life and immortality to light," it surely must have something to tell us about an Intermediate-life, as well as about a more distant Heaven-life; that there must be, somewhere or another in the pages of Holy Writ, a brighter light on the subject than the traditions and theologies of the past had thrown.

Then I felt that it was just possible that the last word had not been spoken by which the truth of God should be better interpreted.

I knew that astronomers in past years had had the same "book of the heavens" as we have, and had failed to read in it great physical truths that

we of to-day can read therein. Could it be possible, I wondered, that in that other book of the
heavens—the Bible—other great truths might exist
that had been overlooked by the theologians of the
past?

I was disturbed by the thought. It seemed to
savour of presumption; to strike a death-blow to
the authority of Church and Chapel Traditionalism.

Yet I could not rid myself of it. It grew upon
me; it became a deeply-rooted conviction that
Christian men, as the ages rolled on, might advance
to clearer perceptions of religious truth, as the men
of science had advanced to clearer perceptions of
physical truth. The Bible, I knew, would not be
altered, but it might be better understood.

The duties of a busy ministerial life in a pop-
ulous London parish deepened this conviction.

Very often I stood at death-beds, and realized
that the commonly-accepted eschatological theology did not rob death of its sting. Many, like
Martha, were not comforted because they knew
that a dear one "shall rise again in the resurrection
t the last day." A living love cried out for some-

thing more than a *dead* object upon which to centre itself.

The words of the Saviour, spoken to the sorrowing sister, fastened themselves upon my mind—" Whosoever liveth and believeth in Me *shall never die*."

What if He meant more than the preachers had taught! What if the only thing that can scare away the horror of dying, be the magnificent truth crystallized in the words of the American poet—

" There is no Death! What seems so is *transition ;* . . .
. . . She *lives*, whom we call dead ! "

Was it possible for me to work out that glorious comfort for myself and others on the sure foundation of Holy Scripture ?

Could I, from the statements of the Sacred Book, show that man after death, and before a distant resurrection, is a being of life and reality, and that more was revealed to us by a gracious Father-God than had "been dreamed of in the philosophy" of many ?

Slowly, but surely, after years of thought and study, the answer came to me, and I think it came from God. This little work is the result.

I commend it to the thoughtful and prayerful consideration of my Christian brothers and sisters in America.

It is not a " Party " book. It deals with a subject in comparison with which party-shibboleths and differences must fade into veriest insignificance.

The fact that among the letters I have received are many from Non-conformists and even Roman Catholics, leads me to think that, although I am a member of the Church of England, the book on that account will not be less acceptable to many of other communions. Some of my readers may be interested in learning that I am writing a companion-work to " Our Life after Death," in order to deal with other important phases of the subject not dealt with in this volume.

ARTHUR CHAMBERS.

The Vicarage,
Brockenhurst,
Hampshire,
England.
November, 1899.

THE SCHEME OF THE TREATISE

PROPOSITION I.

That a person, although dissociated from his earthly body in passing through the experience which we call "Death," still continues to live *as a Conscious Personality,* *36*

9

The bearing of this Deduction upon Christian
thought and experience:—

It is calculated to dispel much of the terror

APPENDIX

Our Life After Death

"*Where* is he? *Where* is she? WHAT is this solemn mystery which those white, sealed lips may not disclose?"

These are questions which we have asked ourselves as we have stood in the darkened death-chamber, and timidly gazed on the rigid, wax-like features of the departed.

And one may be quite sure that these involuntary questionings are not merely indications of an idle curiosity, nor of a morbid craving for the sensational and the unknown.

They have their roots in truer and nobler feelings. They spring from the better side of our nature; from that deeply implanted, and ineradicable instinct which makes it impossible for us to forget, and cease to love, many who, by the transplanting hand of Death, have passed outside the circle of earthly contact and intercourse.

If, within us, there be this yearning affection for a departed one; if, as Christians, we believe that one to be still living, though in a life dissimilar from ours; and if, moreover, we realize that we ourselves are destined, sooner or later, to enter upon the same experience, must it not be impossible, if we are thoughtful, to be other than intensely interested in all that concerns that existence ? Suppose that we were so circumstanced, as to be contemplating a departure from the land of our birth, to rejoin friends who had preceded us to a country strange and unknown, should we not eagerly gather every available scrap of information regarding that country and the conditions of life there ?

In a few years, at most, we shall be leaving the Earth-life, to follow many whom we have known and loved into another experience—the Hades-life. Is it less natural, reasonable and desirable that we should be anxious to know everything which may be known in regard to that Life ? Surely not.

This, I imagine, will be a sufficient answer to

those who, while themselves content with indefiniteness, consider it right to discourage in others the desire to know more concerning a subject of which God has revealed much.

For the most part, Christian teachers and writers, however forcibly and distinctly they may have endeavored to depict the future Heaven-life, have barely mentioned the existence of an Intermediate or Hades-life. And yet the one is as much a fact as the other.

Many, too, who have written and spoken about the latter, have so enshrouded it, as it were, in mental mistiness, that to many it has seemed a vague, unhuman, and unreal existence; a veritable "world of shadows."

It will be my effort to show, in these pages, that this conception of the Hades-life is false and misleading: that it is as *real* a phase of human existence as is the present Earth-life, and as will be the Heaven-life.

In dealing with this subject, I am, of course, aware that I may, perhaps, offend the prejudices of some. That is a danger which threatens any one who steps out of the rut of conventionality. Further, I may be told that because certain doctors of theology have thought otherwise than myself, it is a proof that I am mistaken in my views. To justify such an assumption, a doctrine of human infallibility, as the exclusive endowment of a select few, is necessary.

Lastly, I may lay myself open to the charge of speculating with regard to Divine truth.

In reply to these possible objections, I have but one answer, which I deem quite sufficient, viz., that prejudice, preconception and theology must bow to the authority of Holy Scripture.

That is the position assumed by the Church of England, as expressed in the VI. Article, and to which I loyally subscribe.

All I ask is that what I have to say may be judged by the standard of the Bible. The teachings and opinions of others on the subject should be authoritative only so far as they agree with the Word of God, when correctly translated.

It will be necessary to clear the way for the discussion of this interesting question, by defining clearly what is meant by the word "Hades." Mis-understanding on this point has led to a great deal of erroneous, and essentially unscriptural teaching.

A better understanding of the Scriptures will scare away many of those ugly shadows that over-hang so much of the theology of the past.

THE MEANING OF THE WORD "HADES."

The Greek language contains two words which are used many times in the New Testament—"Gehenna" and "Hades."

"Gehenna," meaning literally, "the valley of Hinnom "—(2 Chron. xxxiii. 6)—a term applied to a spot outside the walls of Jerusalem, where huge fires were constantly kept burning to consume the offal and refuse of the city—was employed by our Lord to figuratively describe the place or condition of punishment into which the wicked and impenitent will pass after judgment.

"Hades" is used to denote the place or condition into which every person enters at the moment of death, in a physically "unclothed," or disembodied

state. From the fact of its being a midway existence between the Earth-life and the future Heaven-
life, it has come to be called by us the "Intermediate-life"; while St. Paul's well-known contrast
between "the things which are *seen*," and "the
things which are *not seen*" (2 Cor. iv. 18), has led
to its also being spoken of as the "Unseen World."

When the Greek New Testament was translated
into English, *one* English word—"Hell"—was, very
unfortunately, made to do service for the two Greek
words named above. "Hell" was used to express
both the place of future punishments, and also the
abode of those, who having departed the Earth-life,
are existing as disembodied spirits, physically disembodied.

As was to be expected, confusion of ideas soon
arose in consequence, and ordinary readers became
bewildered.

Such a passage as Acts ii. 31: "His soul was not
left in Hell," and the clause in the Apostles' Creed—
"He descended into Hell"—instead of being understood as expressing that Christ at His crucifixion
entered into *Hades*, seem to teach that He went

into the place of punishment—Hell; where He never went.

I have known persons refuse to repeat this clause of the Creed, for that very reason.

It were well if our Church removed this antiquated blunder from her Prayer Book.

Let us, then, be quite clear on this matter.   When we meet with the word "Hell" in our English Bible, we must bear in mind that it sometimes stands for "Hell," and sometimes, for "Hades."

Which of the two is intended, can only be determined by referring to the Greek text, or the Revised Edition of our Bible.

Now, I have said that the word "Hades" in the Greek New Testament is used to denote the place, or condition, into which every person passes at the moment of death, in an "unclothed," or disembodied state; *i. e.*, without a *physical* encasement.

The ground upon which we build our certainty that such is the case, is that this was the thought which the word conveyed to the mind of Jews and Greeks who were contemporaneous with the writers of the Books of the New Testament.

We cannot conceive that the sacred writers would have used, *without comment, or modification*, a popular word, around which had crystallized a fixed idea, if they had not intended that idea to be understood by it.

To have adopted a generally accepted word, and to have imported a *new* sense into it, would have been unjustifiable, except that a very clear and explicit statement had been made, at the time, that the new sense was to be understood.

We have an instance which bears upon this point, in the New Testament. In the Fourth Gospel, St. John applies the term "Logos" ("Word") to Christ. At the time he wrote, the term had an established signification, and was current among the philosophers of a certain school. It denoted the most exalted one of a number of created Intelligences, who were supposed to surround the throne of God. This being, besides existing as a *creature*, was imagined as being incapable of contact with matter.

But when St. John called our Lord, "the Logos," he was very careful to explain that he meant the term to convey a very different meaning in its Christian, from what it had hitherto done in its philosophical use.

He shows at once the radical distinction between the two. The "Logos" of St. John, so far from being a *created* being, "was *God*" (John i. 1); and so far from being incapable of contact with matter, "*was made flesh*" (John i. 14).

If the writers of the New Testament, in their use of the word "Hades," had not intended us to understand by it what everybody living in their times understood by it, how came it that they did not exercise care, as St. John did, to guard against any possibility of misinterpretation?

If Jew and Greek were wrong in their belief in an Intermediate-life; if, in other words, the idea conjured up in their mind by the word "Hades" had no basis in fact, our Lord's incorporation of it into His teaching, and the Apostles' and Evangelists' use of it in their writings, without any indication that the meaning of the word had undergone a change in their hands, can only bear one construction. It was calculated to mislead men, and to propagate untruth.

Hence we conclude that when our Lord and the sacred writers used the word "Hades," they meant by it what those whom they addressed understood by it—an Intermediate-life.

It will be necessary and instructive to glance at the views held on this subject by those who lived at the time the New Testament was written.

The Greek Conception of Hades.

The word itself is Grecian, and etymologically signifies, "Something unseen." The idea which the Greeks had was that the spirits or Manes of the dead went, after their burial, into a locality called "Hades." In that abode, the disembodied souls were placed either in the happy fields of Elysium, or in the gloomy realms of Tartarus. In the former, the souls of the virtuous enjoyed themselves, with a lingering regret for the body which had been left behind. In the latter, the wicked were tormented with different degrees of sorrow.

THE JEWISH CONCEPTION OF HADES.

This did not differ materially from the Grecian conception, except that the Jews, unlike the Greeks, held a belief in a final Resurrection, at which the disembodied spirit would again be re-clothed with a body. This state or place they called in the Hebrew "Sheol," and later, when the Greek had become the common tongue, "Hades." Its position, in accordance with Jewish notions and language, was thought to be underground. Josephus tells us that the soul of Samuel, when he appeared to Saul "came *up* fiom Hades." In another place, he tells us that the rationalizing Sadducees "took away the rewards and punishments of the Soul in Hades": while the Pharisees held that "the souls of men were punished or rewarded *under the earth*, according to their practice of virtue or wickedness in life." From the Rabbinical wiitings we are able to gather that the Jews, like the heathens, looked for a state of conscious existence, immediately after death; that in this state were both the just and the unjust; the latter in a state of misery, the former in blissful enjoy-

ment, to which they applied the following terms:
—"Paradise"—"the Garden of Eden"—"Beneath
the throne of glory" and "Abraham's bosom."

Such then, is a brief but correct statement of the
views concerning the Intermediate-life, of both
Jews and Greeks who were contemporaneous with
our Lord and the sacred writers. It is impossible
that He and they could, again and again, have referred to that Life, as I shall show presently they
did, if the thought conveyed by the word had been
but the creation of a fancy, and had no foundation
in fact.

There is nothing in their utterances on this subject to lead us to suppose that this particular teaching was on any different footing from that of their
other teachings, and to say that they were simply
adapting their instruction to popular conceptions
which were untrue, is nothing other than asserting
that they lent themselves to the dissemination of
error.

Hence, we are driven to this conclusion—that the
belief in the Hades-life, as entertained by Jews and
Greeks, is a belief founded on reality, for the reason

that it is sanctioned by Christ and the writers of the New Testament.

THE EARLY-CHRISTIAN CONCEPTION OF HADES.

The foregoing conclusion is well-nigh unassailable, in view of the fact that the early Christians believed in an Intermediate State, which they, like the Jews and Greeks, called "Hades."

Justin Martyr (A. D. 147) declares that "those who say that there is no Resurrection, but that, immediately after death, their souls are taken up to Heaven, these are not to be accounted either Christians or Jews."

Tertullian (A. D. 200) states that "the souls of all men go to Hades until the Resurrection; the souls of the just being in that part of Hades called the 'Bosom of Abraham,' or 'Paradise.'"

Origin (A. D. 230) expresses the same views.

Lactantius (A. D. 306) writes, "Let no one think that souls are judged immediately after death; for they are all detained in the same common place of keeping, until the time come when the Supreme Judge shall enquire into their good or evil deeds."

Hilary (A. D. 350) speaks of its being "the law of human necessity, that bodies should be buried, and souls descend to Hades."

Augustine (A. D. 398) writes—"The time between death and final resurrection holds the souls in hidden receptacles, according as each soul is meet for rest or punishment."

It were easy to multiply, indefinitely, instances as above; but these are sufficient to prove that the belief, held alike by Jews and Greeks, and recognized by our Lord and the sacred writers, gained the acceptance of the early Christian Church.

THE TRUTH ABOUT AN INTERMEDIATE-LIFE INSUFFICIENTLY REALIZED BY MANY CHRISTIANS.

I have especially emphasized the circumstance that our Lord and His disciples emphatically stamped with their authority a belief in the Hades-life, because so many good people, if they do not actually deny it, at least, hardly ever think about it. By many it is not realized, or, at all events, but very faintly, that this truth is an essential portion of the Christian religion.

The fault, I think, lies principally at the door of our teachers and preachers. The subject has been rarely handled in books, and not often is it dealt with from the pulpit. The gaze of Christians has been so earnestly, and not wrongly, directed upon the goal of Christ's Redemption—the future Heaven-life,—that the existence which intervenes between this life and that has been too little regarded, or has altogether been lost to sight. And yet this ought not to be so, if we are desirous of maintaining "the proportion of the faith"; and the fact that it has been so, has been a fruitful cause of error as to *where* we go, and *what* we become, at the moment of death.

The popular idea, happily less prevalent now than formerly, is that when a good person dies, he goes direct to Heaven; and that when a wicked person dies, he passes at once into Hell. Have we not read in books, more distinguished for their piety than scripturalness, many such passages as this? "The dying Christian commended himself to God, and a moment later, the suffering saint of earth was standing before God's throne in *Heaven.*" But it is not true. You may search the Bible from end to end without finding a passage which will justify such a statement.

No one—saint or sinner—passes into Heaven or Hell, on departing from the Earth-life. Not even did our Lord enter Heaven when He died. He was truly Man, as well as truly God, and consequently, had the experience which is allotted to all men. When the lifeless and disfigured Casket hung upon the cross, the emancipated spirit—the real Jesus— passed, at the instant of death, (as our physically unclothed spirits will pass) into the Unseen World —the Hades-life, where are the millions of the departed.

In that Life, the departed, already possessed of a spirit-form, will remain, until one day, in the stead of the physical body laid aside forever at death, they will be super-vested with a new body, spiritual in its constitution, and like unto Christ's glorious Body. Redeemed in body, soul and spirit, they will then, and not until then, enter Heaven, whither the Risen Christ has preceded them. As it was with Christ, so will it be with them: man will

only tread the Courts of Deity wearing Resurrec-
tion-robes.

Consider, for a moment, to what difficulty and
absurdity they commit themselves, who ignore the
fact of an Intermediate-life.

It is taught by many, that, at death, a good man
departs straightway to Heaven, and a wicked man
to Hell. Is it possible to reconcile this idea with
the thought of a Judgment?

Take the case of the wicked. If, in departing
from the Earth-life, they pass direct into Hell,
where is the need of a Judgment? They have been
sent to their doom; nay more, may have had, by
now, thousands of years of punishment, and may
yet suffer, if the Judgment be distant enough, for
double that period before the Day arrives. Will
any one say that it is compatible with either justice
or sense to put such an one *on his trial*, when for
ages before, his doom has been fixed and endured?
Would not a judgment-trial, under such circumstances, be as solemn a farce, as for the law of this
country to send a prisoner into penal servitude, and
then, after he had undergone twenty years of it, to

try him at the Old Bailey for the offence for which
he had been already punished ? The thought is
simply intolerable; and yet to escape it we are
obliged to adopt one of two alternatives. Either
there is, at death, an unconsciousness, or annihila-
tion of the man until a time of Judgment, or there
is an Intermediate-life.

As regards a state of unconsciousness between
death and the Judgment, the utterances of Christ,
St. Peter, and St. Paul, together with the consensus
of belief, Jewish, Grecian, and Christian, for past
centuries, are against it. With regard to an Intermediate-life, the Bible proclaims it, Jesus confirms
it, and our reason approves it.

That Life is Chapter II. of human existence, and
the Judgment will be an incident of that chapter.

THE STATEMENTS OF HOLY SCRIPTURE REGARDING THE
HADES-LIFE.

Let us endeavor, now, to see what light is cast
upon this important subject by the Word of God.
And in doing this, it will be well for us to settle,

beforehand, what kind of testimony may reasonably be expected from this source.

For example, we shall not expect to find in the Bible as much information concerning the Intermediate-life, as about the present Earth-life. And the reason of this is that the Bible has been written rather to teach men how they should live at the *present* time, than to furnish particulars as to *future* existences. The desire of God is that to all who have the Bible "*now*" should be "the accepted time"; "*to-day*, the day of salvation."

As Christians, it is a greater concern to us to learn how we should live now, than how we shall live hereafter; because our future will be an outcome of our present, and the character of the one will be determined by the other. We expect therefore that Holy Scripture will clearly reveal this future existence, and its intimate relationship to our present existence; but we do not expect that the information afforded of the one will be as full as that of the other. A Guide-Book to holiness, addressed to those living in the Earth-life, will necessarily deal more especially with the experiences of the Earth-life. The purpose of the Bible, while, of course, it reveals the future, is not so much to lay bare the details of that future, as to concentrate attention upon the importance of a present, out of which the future will arise.

Again, we shall not look to find, in the Bible, as much stress laid upon the Intermediate-life, as upon the future Heaven-life. But this need not astonish us. It will not do so, if we consider God's twofold purpose in giving men the Holy Scriptures. First, to influence them to the leading of a Christian life; next, to depict for them the *ultimate* issue of such a life.

They stimulate us to a patient plodding along the highroad of holiness, by indicating the Goal which lies at the end of that pathway.

They urge us to a more earnest striving after the prizes of godliness, by showing what the greatest Prize of all will be.

If we wish to incite a son to be earnest in his efforts to attain a coveted position, we are less concerned to fix his gaze upon the intervening experiences through which he must pass on the way to that position, than upon the attractiveness of the position itself.

It is so with the Bible. It dwells more upon the Consummation of a life of holiness and faith, than upon the intervening experience through which men will pass to that Consummation.

That Consummation will be the Heaven-life—the Goal of Christ's Salvation—where, in " spirit, soul and body," man will be " perfect and entire, wanting nothing."

That " intervening experience " will be the Hades-life:—a higher school, but still only a school; a means to an end, but not the end itself.

Need we wonder, then, such being the case, that Holy Scripture should have more to say of the Heaven-life, than of the Hades-life ? The one is but man's sphere of continued discipline and his temporary residence; the other, his Eternal Home.

Our purpose, then, is to ascertain what the Bible has to say with respect to this Intermediate Existence. And we shall see that its teaching establishes the three following main propositions.

PROPOSITION I.

That a person, although dissociated from his earthly body in passing through the experience which we call "death," still continues to live as a Conscious Personality.

Scripture adduces three historical instances of this truth.

The persons referred to had departed the Earth-life, but are, nevertheless, introduced into a sober, matter-of-fact narration of earthly events, as *living*, *thinking* and *speaking* individuals.

No question as to their having departed the Earth-life is possible. The body of one had been in the grave four years; that of another had crumbled into dust centuries before; while the Body of the Third lay lifeless and lacerated in a seeled-up sepulchre.

The first is the prophet Samuel. Four years after death, he the *living man*, at the bidding of the woman of Endor, confronts the guilty, panic-stricken Saul, and speaks to him.

The second is Moses. Apart from the thronging

multitude, but in sight of wondering disciples, he, physically bodiless for ages, steps from out the Unseen World to hold converse with Christ on the Mount of Transfiguration, so real, and manlike in his spirit-form, that St. Peter wanted to make a tabernacle for him.

The third is the Master Himself, and the writer to whom we are indebted for the account is St. Peter, who saw Moses on the Mount of Transfiguration. He tells us in his Epistle (1 Peter iii. 18–20) that when the Body of Jesus was stiffening in death on the cross, the departed Tenant was preaching unto "spirits," who had departed this life in a state of disobedience.

All three of these persons had died; all had left behind the earthly body, and yet they stand forth on the page of Divine Inspiration as *living*, *thinking* and *speaking*.

Take, now, our Lord's utterances in support of this proposition.

In His parable of Lazarus and Dives (Luke xvi. 19–31), both men are represented as having died. "The beggar died . . . the rich man also died."

And yet, after death, both are depicted as living, thinking and speaking.

On another occasion, when disputing with the Sadducees who denied an After-life, He sought to convince them that Abraham, Isaac and Jacob, though they had departed the Earth-life ages before, were still living, because God had said, "I *am* (not I *was*) the God of Abraham," etc. This argument He followed up by saying, "For he is not a God of the dead; but of the *living ;* for all *live* unto Him" (Luke xx. 38).

Again, in His words, "Fear not them which kill the body, but are not able to kill the soul" (Matt. x. 28), the inference is unmistakable. By "the soul" is meant that Ego, or Consciousness—the spirit encased in its spirit-body—which is capable of surviving the catastrophe which destroys the physical body. There are those who contend that the word "soul" in Scripture, means nothing more than the principle of *physical life.* If this be so, then our Lord's words confront them with this difficulty, that those which kill the physical body are *not* able to kill the physical life. Assuredly a self-evident absurdity.

There are many other passages (notably Phil. i. 23 and 24; 2 Cor. v. 1–4 and 6–8) which could be adduced to establish the fact that our consciousness —our self—is maintained in and beyond death; but as I shall have occasion to refer to them in dealing with another phase of this subject, the foregoing will suffice for our first proposition.

PROPOSITION II.

That a person, while maintaining his Conscious Personality in and through the incident of death, does not THEN continue his existence in either HEAVEN or HELL.

In other words, neither of those two spheres of existence is entered on leaving the Earth-life. It has already been indicated that much misunderstanding exists upon this point. Our hymns and religious writings are conspicuous in this respect for their unscripturalness.

In the Bible, Heaven and Hell are always depicted as *future* existences; as experiences of enjoyment or unhappiness which are *to follow* the Judgment. It never represents that either the one or the other condition will be entered at the moment of bodily dissolution.

The teaching of our Lord most emphatically confirms this. Over and over again He stated that the determining event of a man's future experience will be the Judgment. *Then* he will pass to reward or punishment. *Then* he will enter Heaven or Hell. "The Son of Man shall come in the glory of His Father, with His angels; and *then* He shall reward every man according to his works" (Matt. xvi. 27).

A number of like passages (*e. g.*, Matt. xiii. 40–43; xxv. 31–46; John v. 28 and 29) show how unwarranted is the idea that at the moment of death a good man enters Heaven, or a bad man, Hell. But even more convincing than these passages are some other words of Christ, the force of which it is impossible to explain away. He said, "No one hath ascended up to Heaven, but He that came down from Heaven, even the Son of Man which is in Heaven" (John iii. 13) If, then, no one had then ascended up to Heaven except the Lord Jesus, who had come from there, none of the good men who had departed the Earth-life before He came could have gone to their place of final and eternal bliss, which is always called Heaven. And yet, as Christ showed, they were living. Where? Again, our Lord told the thief on the cross that "he should be with Him that day in Paradise" (Luke xxiii. 43). Now, it is quite certain that Christ did not go from the cross to Heaven, but passed, as we shall see later, in a physically disembodied state, into the Hades-life. Even after His Resurrection He said to Mary, "I am *not yet* ascended to My Father" (John xx. 17). Therefore, the "Paradise" to which the thief went with Him, on the day of the crucifixion, was not Heaven.

There is another important passage which we cannot pass over without notice in this connection. In Rev. vi. 9, 10, "the souls of them that were slain for the word of God," are represented as crying from "under the altar," for justice against those who had wronged them in the Earth-life. That the expression "under the altar," does not denote "Heaven" is quite plain; first, for the reason that its established usage bore an altogether different sig-nification, as we shall see; and next, that the condition of those mentioned as being there, is incompatible with the restfulness, satisfaction and perfection which will characterize the Heaven-life.

In like manner, Holy Scripture is equally emphatic in pronouncing that no one, at the moment of death, passes into Hell.

Neither our Lord, nor His apostles, threaten the wicked that *at dying* their souls will enter at once into the punishment of Hell.

It is to a Judgment and to what will follow it, that the gaze of the ungodly is directed.

To what, then, are we to attribute the fact that so many excellent Christians have held and taught a doctrine the opposite of this? To the unfortunate circumstance to which we have already alluded; viz., that the one English word "Hell" has been used to translate two Greek words of completely different meanings. Passages in the English Authorized Version of the New Testament using the word "Hell" are flatly contradicted by the corresponding passages of the Greek New Testament. The inaccuracy of the translators, in this case as in several others, has begotten a theological falsehood.

PROPOSITION III.

That a person, maintaining his conscious personality in and through death, enters at once into an Intermediate, or Hades-life.

In considering this phase of our subject, we will take, first, our Lord's own words in connection therewith. If He came as the Divine Revealer of man's future, it is incredible, if an Intermediate-life be a fact, that He should not disclose that fact. Moreover, if such a Life had no existence save in the minds of poets and mistaken theologians, surely He, as the expounder of truth, was under the obligation to explode the fallacy.

Did He, then, in clear and unequivocal language, bear testimony to the truth of the Hades-life?

He did. Take His parable of Lazarus and Dives, and His words spoken to a man on the eve of passing into that Life.

In the parable, the beggar and the rich man are not only portrayed as living personalities, after having passed through the experience of death, but the sphere in which their existence is continued is named. "It came to pass that the beggar died, and was carried by the angels into *Abraham's bosom.* The rich man also died and was buried; and in Hades he lifted up his eyes" (Luke xvi. 22, 23).

Now, the expression, "Abraham's bosom," as has been already stated, was a term common among the Jews to describe that part of Hades into which the righteous pass at death. It is frequently employed by the Rabbinical writers, and is never confounded with the Heaven-life which will follow the Resurrection.

Our Lord, in using this expression, most certainly intended that meaning to be taken, because the Jews whom He addressed attached no other meaning to it.

Clearly, then, Lazarus was in *Hades.*

Our English New Testament represents the rich man as being in *Hell.* But the translation is a false one. In the original Greek it is, "In *Hades* he lifted up his eyes."

So, then, the rich man, though in another sphere than that of Lazarus, was also in Hades. I am aware that some teachers have viewed this parable as depicting the future condition of man, in happiness or misery, in *Heaven* or *Hell*. But besides the locality in which the two persons are placed being actually named, the context is against such a supposition. At the time that Lazarus and Dives are shown in their after-death experiences, this world is still in existence, and the brothers of the rich man are then living on the earth, and the Judgment is still distant. But Heaven and Hell will *follow*, not *precede*, the close of the present Dispensation and the Judgment. We conclude, therefore, that this parable distinctly affirms the truth of an Intermediate-life.

We come, now, to Christ's words spoken to the dying robber. "To-day shalt thou be with Me in Paradise" (Luke xxiii. 43). Conjure up the scene as conveyed by the brief narrative. A wretched, pain-racked man, with the awful shadow of death falling upon him, turns his haggard eyes upon his fellow-sufferer, and with his spiritual perception quickened by the near approach of eternity, asks Him to "remember him" at that future time when He shall come into His Kingdom. The answer

which comes from the pitiful Saviour of mankind
scatters the terrors of death, and soothes the agony
of dying. He has pleaded for a blessing in the
future ; Christ will give him one *at once.* "Verily,
I say unto thee," said Jesus, "*to-day* shalt thou be
with Me in Paradise." What signification did the
word "Paradise" bear to the dying man? No
other, surely, than it conveyed to all Jews. It described with several other terms, as we have seen,
the lot of the righteous in Hades. The robber himself was, undoubtedly, a Jew, as his death by crucifixion rather than by decapitation indicates. In
using that word, Jesus knew perfectly well the
meaning the man would attach to it.

Why did He transfer that sufferer's gaze from the
future, and fix it upon the *present*, unless the present were a reality ?

Both Jesus and the robber were on the point of
stepping out of the Earth-life, and it is difficult to
conceive of a more solemn attestation to the existence of an Intermediate-life than is afforded by
these words.

From the testimony of Christ as to the Hades-life,

we pass now to the testimony of the Apostles. And it is very significant that the Apostles, into whose writings the subject is introduced, were men who were personally brought into contact with the Hades-life.

St. Peter and St. John saw and heard Moses when he stepped from out that Life to converse with Christ on the Mount of Transfiguration; while St. Paul had the absolutely unique experience of entering into the Hades-life before the axe of Nero had terminated his earthly existence.

St. Peter's Testimony.

The passage is 1 Peter iii. 18–20, and is exceedingly valuable as showing *where* our Lord was during the period between crucifixion and resurrection.

It confirms entirely the sense which we have insisted must be placed upon the word "Paradise," and which is embodied in the clause of the Creed, "He descended into Hades." We give the passage as it stands in the original. "Christ . . . having been put to death in the flesh, but quickened in the spirit; in which (*i. e.*, in His spirit-condition)

also He went and preached unto the spirits in prison
(or ' *keeping* ') who once were disobedient." The
translators have obscured this passage by substituting the word "by" for "in," and by putting a
capital " S " to the word " Spirit."

If any reliability whatever is to be placed upon
language, these words can only mean that the disembodied Christ went into a sphere where other
disembodied spirits were, and preached to them.
That this is the sense intended is plain from what
St. Peter says in the next chapter. " For for this
cause was the Gospel preached also to them that
are dead, (*i. e,*. to the departed) that they might be
judged according to (*i. e.*, by the same standard as)
men in the flesh, but live according to God in the
spirit" (1 Peter iv. 6).

These two passages establish incontrovertibly
three points. Firstly—That our Lord, after death,
and before His Ascension, preached to "spirits."
Secondly—That these " spirits " had left the Earth-
life, as indicated by the words " them that are
dead," which refer to their *bodily* condition, for
there would be no sense in preaching to lifeless

beings. Thirdly—That these "spirits" were certainly not in Heaven or Hell, because the preaching was in view of a Judgment that had not yet taken place, and Heaven and Hell will *follow* that.

This preaching to sinners in Hades was predicted by our Lord, when He said, "The hour is coming, and *now is,* when the dead (*i. e.*, the departed) shall hear the voice of the Son of God" (John v. 25).

Hence we are driven to the conclusion that St. Peter teaches the existence of an Intermediate-life, and that into that Life Jesus and the robber passed at the moment of death. The One to preach; the other to listen.

St. John's Testimony.

This Apostle is quite as emphatic as St. Peter in his witness to the truth of a Hades-life. There are several references to it in the last book of the New Testament, and the character of the writing, as being a revelation accorded to him, lends additional weight to his utterances It will be necessary to glance at one or two passages.

In Rev. i. 18, are these words, "I am alive for

evermore, Amen; and have the keys of Hell, and of death." The word "Hell," in the Greek, is "Hades."

Again, in Rev. xx. 12 and 13. "I saw the dead small and great stand before God; and the books were opened; and another book was opened, which is the book of life: and the dead were judged out of those things which were written in the books, according to their works. And the sea gave up the dead which were in it; and death and Hell (Greek: '*Hades*') delivered up the dead which were in them." Surely these words contain the doctrine of an Intermediate-life, and teach that neither the realm of physical Death which seems to claim the departed ("the dead"), nor the World of Hades which holds their spirits, can hinder man from standing at the bar of Judgment.

At that Judgment, the Hades-life will be superseded either by the Heaven-life, or by that awful punishment—Hell; which latter will darken creation as long as sin endures, and until the last sinner, saved "so as by fire," shall have bent in penitence at a Heavenly Father's feet, and sought for pardon and restoration.

We have already referred to those other pregnant words of St. John—"I saw under the altar the souls of them that were slain for the word of God" (Rev. vi. 9).

They need only be recalled in order to point out that the expression, "under the altar," was another of several Jewish phrases denoting the place or condition of the righteous in Hades.

St. John was a Jew, and used a Jewish expression without so much as a hint of any other than the generally accepted meaning being intended. The inference is plain.

St. Paul's Testimony.

This, as that of the two last-named Apostles, is very clear and convincing.

Before instancing the passages in which St. Paul refers to the Hades-life, let us endeavor to form some idea of the Apostle's attitude toward that truth.

One fact lies patent to every thoughtful reader of his Epistles. It is this: That his gaze was intently and preeminently fixed upon the *Consummation* of

Christ's Salvation, viz., the Resurrection, and the Heaven-life which will start from it. Compared with that, every other experience through which he was passing, or would pass, paled into comparative insignificance. Grand and attractive as was the Intermediate-life to him, when wearied with hardship and burdened with care, still it would not be the Perfected-life. Grateful as it would have been to him to be "unclothed" from the "tabernacle" of a body enfeebled by ill-health, he, with his eye set upon the crowning act of redemption—"to wit the redemption of our body" (Rom. viii. 23), was nevertheless constrained to write, "not that we would be unclothed, but clothed upon" (2 Cor. v. 4).

Certain, as he was, of there being the nearer Presence of Christ in the Intermediate-life, so that he could say, "We are confident and willing rather to be absent from the body, and to be present with the Lord" (2 Cor. v. 8), yet, even that thought did not weaken the absorbing desire "to be *clothed upon* with our house which is from Heaven" (2 Cor. v. 2).

Our concern, then, is to show that, while the splendor and glory of the future Heaven-life eclipsed the attractiveness of the Intermediate-life, and caused St. Paul to say less of the latter than of the former, yet he distinctly affirmed the existence of this Intermediate-life. This will be seen from the following passages:—

"For we that are in this tabernacle do groan, being burdened; not that we would be unclothed, but clothed upon, that mortality might be swallowed up of life" (2 Cor. v. 4).

"Knowing that whilst we are at home in the body, we are absent from the Lord" (v. 6).

"Willing rather to be absent from the body, and to be present with the Lord" (v. 8).

"I am in a strait betwixt two, having a desire to depart, and to be with Christ: which is far better; nevertheless, to abide in the flesh is more needful for you" (Phil. i. 23, 24).

Let us grasp the import of these passages.

First —That the "we" expresses persons altogether distinct from the "tabernacle" in which they may happen to dwell This is unquestionable, be-

cause in 2 Cor. v. 1 the Apostle calls this "tabernacle" "our earthly *house*," and no one will say
that a house and its tenant are identical.

Secondly.—That the "we" are capable of *three*
phases of experience:—

(*a*) "We that are *in this tabernacle*," *i. e.*, en-
closed in a physical body; answering to the Earth-
life.

(*b*) We that might be "*unclothed*," *i. e.*, physically disembodied; denoting the Hades-life.

(*c*) We that would be "*clothed upon*," *i. e*, re-
vested with a Resurrection-body—a body not
physical, but spiritual, in its structure; predicating
the future Heaven-life.

Thirdly.—Being "present with the Lord" is associated with being "absent from the body."

This presence with Christ cannot refer to the
Heaven-life, because there we shall not be absent
from the body. We shall then be in possession of
a Resurrection-body. We shall have been "clothed
upon."

It can only, then, point to a condition of physical
disembodiment; in other words, to the Intermedi-

ate-life. That there can be a Presence of Christ there, is perfectly clear from the circumstance that He promised it to the dying robber.

Two passages from the Epistle to the Hebrews must next claim our notice.

St. Paul (assuming him to be the writer of this Epistle), in addressing Christians, says, "Ye are come unto Mount Sion, and unto the city of the living God, the Heavenly Jerusalem, and to an innumerable company of angels, to the general assembly and church of the first-born, which are written in Heaven, and to God, the Judge of all, and to *the spirits* of just men made perfect" (Heb. xii. 22 and 23).

The entire passage shows that he is referring to the present, and not to any future time. He does not say ye *shall* come, but "*are* come," and proceeds to enumerate what was *then existing*. In this enumeration are "the *spirits* of just men." But where? Surely not in the Heaven-life. That was still distant, and the Apostle is speaking of what is present; and moreover, the word "spirits" presupposes the non-possession of the celestial embodiment, which is not a characteristic of the Heaven-life.

If, then, these "spirits of just men" were at that time existing, though not in the Heaven-life, where were they? Only one answer is possible. They were in the Intermediate-life.

This inference is confirmed by another passage in the same Epistle. The Apostle has recounted the triumphs of faith, and referring to a long list of departed worthies, writes, "These all, having obtained a good report through faith, received not the promise: God having provided some better thing for us, that they without us *should not be made perfect*" (Heb. xi. 40).

What does he mean by the words, "*not* made perfect"? In the first of these two passages he has spoken of "spirits of just men *made perfect.*" In both cases he is referring to the departed. Is he then contradicting himself? Not at all. He is simply teaching that the perfecting of the Interme-diate-life is a perfecting which concerns only the *spirits* of men—a perfecting of character and nature. There is another perfecting which will come only with the Resurrection—the reclothing of man with an immortal spiritual body. The perfecting of the spirit takes place in the Hades-life; but man, in spiritual bodily form, will not be like his glorified Saviour until after that.

Now, inasmuch as St. Paul described these departed worthies as "not made perfect," it is evident that he intends us to view them as still remaining "unclothed" in the Hades-life. They were awaiting their investiture of the spiritual-body.

Only one other passage remains for our consideration. It is a very important one.

In 2 Cor. xii. 2–4, St. Paul writes, "I knew a man in Christ above fourteen years ago, (whether in the body, I cannot tell; or whether out of the body, I cannot tell; God knoweth;) such an one caught up to the third heaven. And I knew such a man, (whether in the body, or out of the body, I cannot tell; God knoweth;) how that he was caught up into Paradise, and heard unspeakable words, which it is not lawful for a man to utter."

It is obvious that the words, "I knew a man," refer to the Apostle himself. His statement in the

preceding verse, " It is not expedient for *me*, doubtless, to glory. I will come to visions and revela-
tions of the Lord," makes this evident. Besides,
we can hardly imagine that, had the person been
other than himself, St. Paul would not have been
able to distinguish the difference between a departed
spirit, and a being still in a body of flesh. The
" man," then, was the Apostle himself, and his
reason for suppressing his name was, as the context
shows, to avoid all appearance of boasting. Notice,
next, that the experience into which he entered
while yet connected with the Earth-life, in no way
impaired his conscious personality. Twice he says
" Whether in the body, or out of the body, I cannot
tell." Of one thing he was quite certain, that
whether, or not, he had carried his physical body
with him into that experience, he could yet think,
see, hear and understand. His knowledge that
man possesses, even when encased in flesh, an interior spirit-form or organization, which can act
independently of the physical organization, caused
him to be in doubt as to whether in this experience
he was on the plane of the physical or the spiritual.

Further, he names the place into which he was
" caught up "—" Paradise."

It is impossible to mistake the import of his
words. He, a Jew, employs a well-known Hebrew
term which his Master Himself had used. And
that term denoted the Hades-World.

The passage is the record of an experience vouchsafed to comparatively few. St. Paul, doubtless,
without his physical body, was taken, before his
Earth-life was finished, into Paradise—the Intermediate-life. Perhaps the reason why he, while
yet the tenant of an "earthly house," was permitted to visit a World into which others are not
usually permitted to enter until the time of death,
was that his grasp upon eternal truths might be the
greater. Certainly his subsequent writings indicate
that this result had been effected. As to this experience having taken place *before* death, surely it
is conceivable that, as Lazarus at the bidding of
Christ could reinhabit a body which had died, so
St. Paul, at a like bidding, could have been tem-
porarily separated from a body which may have
been in a condition of sleep or trance.

This, then, constitutes the review of the passages in Holy Scripture, which establish the truths embodied in the three foregoing propositions, viz., that man, although deprived by death of his earthly body, survives his change of condition, as a conscious personality, and continues his existence, not in Heaven, or Hell, but in the Intermediate-life.

Other truths concerning the Hades-life which may be deduced from the foregoing and other statements of Holy Scripture.

The passages brought forward in support of our three main propositions suggest, if they do not explicitly state, a great deal more than is embraced in those propositions.

It will be our task, now, to discover what deductions we may fairly and honestly draw from these inspired utterances.

DEDUCTION I.

That there will be no break in the continuity of our existence in passing from the Earth-life to the Hades-life.

There will be no losing of one's self at death, and after an interval of oblivion, a re-starting of existence under new conditions. Chapter II. of human experience is not the commencement of a new history. It is but the continuation of Chapter I. The one life merges into the other, just as the infant-life merges into the boy-life, and the boy-life into the man-life. The underlying principle, the Consciousness,—the Ego—which existed in the infant-life, passed untouched into the boy-life, and is continued in the man-life.

It is so with our self—our Ego—in its passage from the Earth-life to the Hades-life. However different the sphere of existence may be, our self will be the same. There will be no gap in our consciousness. I shall be as much *myself* when divested of my body, as I am when stripped of my coat. Death will not change my being, but only its environment. The drawing of my last breath will not make me, practically, *another* being with a different set of thoughts, feelings, impulses and emotions. It will simply usher me into another condition of life as the same " I."

As we shall leave off at the close of the Earth-life, we shall begin in the Hades-life.

Is this the teaching of the Bible? Yes. The prophet Samuel revisits earth from the Unseen World. He had the shape, the voice, and the thoughts of a man. He is the same Samuel. He talks to Saul almost word for word as he had been wont to converse with him before leaving the Earth-life.

The Samuel of earth, and the Samuel of Hades was the same person, unchanged by death, except that the grosser body was gone, and his horizon of experience enlarged.

Moses talks with the world's Redeemer on a mountain of northern Palestine. He is very real, and St. Peter, with his Jewish instincts, identifies, at once, the visitant who has come, he knows not whither, as the great departed Lawgiver of his people. It is the same Moses who had once dwelt on earth, with a similar bent of mind, and feelings. In the Earth-life, his thoughts had been concentrated on the sacrificial system of the Levitical Dispensation. Our glimpse of him as he steps from out the

Hades-life, shows him to be still thinking in the same groove. The thought of sacrifice was still uppermost, for St. Luke tells us that he spake of Christ's *decease* which should be accomplished at Jerusalem. There had been no break in the consciousness and mind which had been transferred from Earth to Hades.

Again, the words of our Lord to the dying robber teach the same truth. The position of the adverb, "To-day," in the sentence, in the Greek, indicates that the writer intended it to be emphatic. The dying men upon the crosses, within a few hours, were to pass from one world to another, but with their consciousness unimpaired: "To-day, *thou*, to whom I am speaking, shalt be with *Me*, the Being who is addressing thee, in Paradise."

Once more, St. Paul, with his intense individuality, his exalted feelings, and devotion to his Lord, had "a desire to depart." But can we think that he would have had that desire, unless he had been absolutely convinced that in being with Christ in the "unclothed" Life, he would remain the *same* Paul, unchanged in his sentiments? In spite of the

hardships of his Earth-life, he so rejoiced in the
sense of his Master's presence as to write, "To me
to live is Christ" (Phil. i. 21).   Yet in the next line,
he added, "To die is gain."   But how so, unless
the mind and faculties by which he enjoyed Christ
were to pass uninjured through the ordeal of dying?
If death was capable of denuding him of his power
of thinking, loving, and enjoying, so far from its
becoming a gain to him, it would be a direct loss.
Nor will any consideration of his blissful lot in a
distant future alter the fact.

May we not, therefore, conclude from such texts
as the above, that in undergoing the experience of
dying, our Self will persist untouched and un-
harmed?

And what is the Self?   Not, assuredly, our physical body, except we be prepared to admit that the
loss of a limb entails a corresponding diminishing
of our individuality.   If I should be less a conscious
being with one arm than I am with two, then, of
course, the disintegration and dissolution of my
whole body may mean the loss of *myself*.   But my
body and my Self are not one and the same.   My

Self is a living spirit—a Consciousness—which thinks, feels, perceives and understands; clothed with a *form*, indeed, but a form less coarse than my outer bodily form, which latter is its encasement in the Earth-life. The soul is the spiritual man plus this spirit-form. Changes and disasters which may befall the physical encasement of a soul while on the earth-plane do not, necessarily, affect the Self who inhabits it. An earthquake may lay a building in ruins; but the destruction of the tenant is not inevitably involved. It may only cause a change of residence.

It is so with regard to our Self—our soul—and our body.

The latter may experience many and great changes, and at last, its great disaster—death. But the Self will survive them all.

This is a truth to which science bears witness.

The particles which compose our body are in a condition of continual ebb and flow.

So much so, that in less than seven years the whole bodily structure has been dissolved and re-modelled. And in the case of a man of fifty, this demolition and rebuilding has taken place at least seven times.

Yet the person himself has persisted through it all. This may be easily enough proved by any one, however unskilled in science.

Cast your mind back over past years. You can remember a circumstance which happened thirty, forty, or fifty years ago. What has occurred during the interval? Your brain, and your whole bodily organization in every particle has been changed over and over again. As far as your body is concerned, not one atom of it existed, as such, when that circumstance took place. Moreover, you are quite sure that you, remembering the event, are the identical person who years ago experienced it. All the argument in the world would not convince you to the contrary. But how can this be, unless you—your real Self— have existed through all those years, and all those changes?

Now, Holy Scripture only supplements what Science affirms about our Self's power of persistence. It tells us that when the greatest change of

all—death—shall come, we who have before survived so many changes, shall survive that also, and
without a break in the continuity of our existence
pass into the Hades-life.

It will not be uninstructive to note the bearing
upon Christian thought and experience of this Deduction and others, which we shall make from the
foregoing statements of Scripture.

The bearing of this, our first, as to there being
no break in the continuity of our existence in
passing from the Earth–life to the Hades-life.

It is calculated to dispel much of the terror with
which Death is regarded by even sincere Chris-
tians.

However deeply rooted our belief in a Hereafter,
there is, in the case of all, a shrinking from the
thought of dying. It is natural that it should be so.
Besides the pain which attends the wrenching of
one's self from his physical encasement, there is
that feeling of strangeness which must accompany
an entrance upon a new environment, and, moreover, the regret at being dissociated from so much

which by long familiarity has become endeared to us. This latter, perhaps, more than anything else, constitutes the pang of dying.

Christ's Gospel has robbed death of its deadliest sting, and irradiated it with hope; but dying, nevertheless, involves, at least for a time, an existence apart from those whose life has hitherto been interwoven with our life. And there must be an element of grief in this, unless our religion has dehumanized us.

I am aware there are some who will tell us that a sincere Christian should long to die, and that if he does not experience that inclination, it is a sure indication that there is something spiritually amiss with him. I am afraid that I can only view such utterances as being the outcome of unreality, for the reason that I have known persons sing, with very great unction, hymns which represent the singer as panting for death, who, nevertheless, when a cold has been contracted, have evinced the greatest terror at the bare prospect of the Almighty taking them at their word.

I do not say that under no circumstances is it

conceivable that one may wish to die. Under great hardship, or intense mental and bodily suffering, many have desired to do so; St. Paul among the number. I have stood at death-beds, and heard the pain-racked sufferer pray for death, and thought it no wrong to kneel down and join in that petition. There has been sincerity in such prayers, wrung as they have been from the depths of human distress.

But if any person in comparative health, and under tolerable circumstances, were to profess to me that he wished to die, so far from accounting it an indication of exalted spirituality, I should view it as being a proof that he stood in need of medical treatment.

We chide our boy who grumbles at his school-life, and imagines that he would like to leave it. Are they less deserving of censure, who by an assumed impatience to get out of the Earth-life, make but a sorry acknowledgment to God for His gift of the same ?

The truth is, no one, except under very exceptional circumstances, can restrain a shudder at the thought of dying. Not even our Lord Himself was unmoved by the approach of death.   And although, in the hour of actual dissolution, there will be vouchsafed to every Christian man, as there was to Christ, an upholding and an uplifting of the spirit, by which all dread of death will vanish; yet until that hour shall come, more or less defined, the dread will exist.

In this way, the Christian's anticipations of death, will, unlike those of his subsequent experiences, be in excess of his realizations.

But this natural shrinking at the thought of death is a very different thing from living in *terror* of it. The one will add a sobering complexion to our life; the other will embitter it.   The one will make us thoughtful; the other, miserable.   The one is a timidity which a closer contact will remove; the other an aversion which nearness will but intensify.

There are many sincerely good persons who are terribly appalled at the prospect of death.   There is no need that we should think them the less Christian on account of this.   Their terror will, most certainly, vanish when they come to die.   They have God's distinct promise that it shall be so.

But while the event is short of actual occurrence, it flings an awful shadow upon their life. Why is this? Because of the physical pain which will attend it? Hardly so, since many a person with a terror of death, will courageously face a suffering compared with which that of dying is light. Is it because it will involve for a time a separation from those dearest to us? This, after all, is only akin to the experience of one who may have to leave home and friends for a distant part of the world. It may produce regret; it cannot evoke terror. Is it, then, because death is unilluminated by hope, and there is no expectation of a Resurrection and a Heaven? No; both may be looked for; but they are *future* facts—how future, is not known—and meanwhile, *what?* Nothing definite. No intense conviction of the unbroken continuity of life. No certainty that the moment after death we shall be the same living, thinking and feeling personalities that we have been the moment before.

No thought that when that solemn scene will be enacted at an open grave, into which our body will be committed, we—our real Selves—*shall be living,* and for all we know to the contrary, may perhaps, be listeners to our Church's grand words of Resurrection and *Life*.

It is the absence of this definiteness concerning the Life after Death which invests dying with such terrors. Tell me that, at the moment of dissolution, I shall lose my consciousness; that there will be a gap in my existence; that I shall, practically, pass into nothingness, until a Resurrection-morning, and I shiver at the thought of being thus chloroformed by Death. Tell me that there *is* an Unseen Life; but, at the same time, that it is dim and shadowy; nebulous and intangible; a world of strangeness and unreality, and I dread the knock of Death which will summon me to such a sphere.

But on the other hand, make the Hades-life what the Bible shows it to be—a real life; an unbroken continuance of a life commenced on earth; a life where I shall be the *same* man as I am now—and oh ! what a different aspect will Death bear. No longer will it be "the king of Terrors." The realization of that Life will denude him of his power to appall me.

Pain and distress may be his ministers in attendance, but they will be but the officers who strike off the chains which bind me down to earth; the birth-pangs, by which I—my real Self—shall pass from the womb of the material to the life of the Spiritual.

The realization, then, of the truth that the passing from the Earth-life to the Hades-life will involve no break in the continuity of our existence, will remove our terror of death.

I shall not, indeed, before the time arrives for me to do so, want to die, because God has appointed me to live awhile in the Earth-life, and many a beloved companion, and many a circumstance make the Lower-school in which God is training me very dear. But when the time shall come for me to enter the "Higher-school"—the Intermediate-life, I shall not, I think, be distressed; certainly I shall not be appalled. My Self will undergo no change, except that of environment. And when God shall have cut away the ropes which moor me to earth, possessed of my thoughts and feelings, my love and desires, I shall learn that for my Self "there is no death, what seems so is transition."

DEDUCTION II.

That in the Hades-life we shall recognize, and be brought into relationship with those whom we have previously known in the Earth-life.

If, as we have endeavored to show, we shall be, in the Intermediate-World, the same living, thinking and speaking beings as on earth, what will constitute an important factor in the continuity of our life in that sphere ?

The reestablishment of intercourse between ourselves and those with whom we have before been in contact.

We may, perhaps, never have reflected that *how* we think and feel; *how* we regard things; and *how* the tone and complexion has been imparted to our character, is very greatly due to our intercourse with others. In the moral universe, as in the physical world, an independent existence is impossible.

For example. You have a certain attribute, or quality, called love; it may be for wife, parent, child, or friend. It is part of your consciousness, and consequently, part of your Self.   Take it away,

and you will have got rid of part of that Self.
Without it, you will be less a consciousness than
you would be with it, in the same way as a body
wanting a limb, will be less a body than another in
which the defect does not exist.

You have another quality called friendship. Take
that away, too, and you will have got rid of still
more of your consciousness—of your Self. Go on
with the process; get rid, one after another, of all
the distinctive attributes of your character, and at
last, you will become, practically, *another* being.
There would be no more sense in calling you, then,
the *same* being, than there would be in describing a
watch as the *same* watch, after the removal of its
old interior. You might substitute a new set of
works for the old; but it would be no longer the
same watch.

This is perfectly in harmony with the utterance
of Scripture. When a man devoid of certain spiritual instincts, becomes possessed of them, and enters upon the Christian life, he is described as "a
new creature." The new world of thought and aspiration into which he enters, in turning to Christ,

has no connection with the old moral world in which he had formerly moved.

In his thoughts and feelings, as a Christian, he is not the *same* being, as he was when an unbeliever.

By a like reasoning, if we are to continue the same in our consciousness, in the Hades-life, as we have been, in the Earth-life, it must follow that we shall take with us, there, our love, friendships and sympathy—in a word, all that makes us what we are.

But from what did these qualities of our Self arise? From contact and intercourse with others. I should never have loved as a husband, but for a wife; nor as a father, but for a child; nor as a son, but for a parent; nor as a friend, but for a companion. If I had had no contact with sorrowful ones, I should never have experienced sympathy; and had there been no association with Christlike men and women, I should have had but a poor appreciation of goodness.

My *entire* consciousness will pass into the Hades-life, and consequently, my love, friendship and sympathy, for these are parts of it.

They came into existence and continued as parts
of me, because of my contact with others.   Are
those others to be unrecognized and unknown by
me there?   It is difficult to believe it.   Were it so,
how can I be sure that my Self (at all events as far
as concerns my love and sympathy) will remain the
same?   The noblest and purest of all love is a
mother's love.   But it owes its origin to, and main-
tains its intensity by, contact with the child.   In
the Hades-life, would the love remain were the
child unrecognized?

Moreover, may not the renewal, in that life, of
intercourses which have been interrupted by Death,
be the very means employed by God for rekin-
dling in us many a noble quality which has grown
to be feeble and attenuated, from want of contact
with the one who had been instrumental in calling
it into being?   It may be, you are a parent, and
loved years ago, a child.   But God took him from
you, and because the intercourse was broken, the
quality of love within you became in after years
less marked than of old.   But what, if when you
step into the Spiritual World, a renewed contact

with your child should cause the smouldering embers to leap into a flame!

Long ago, the noble glow of unselfish friendship irradiated your character. But your friend died, and since then there has been a coldness and a reserve in your manner. But what if in the Hades-life the old loving familiarity be restored, and the glow break forth once more!

It would seem an intolerable thought that the Almighty Father should allow our being to be·so interwoven with that of others, as that they should have been instrumental in evoking, determining, and maintaining our thoughts, feelings, and impulses, and then, that He should not let us know them in the Hades-life.

You may crowd that Life with troops of resplendent angels, and throng its "many mansions" with "spirits of just men made perfect"; but, methinks, I shall pass them all by, and be uninterested and unsatisfied, until I shall meet there those whom "I have loved long since, and lost awhile."

Have we a basis in Holy Scripture, for such belief? Yes.

Disembodied Samuel was recognized both by the woman of Endor, and by the guilty King, at whose bidding she had summoned the departed prophet to Earth again.

Disembodied Moses was identified as the great departed Lawgiver, by the Apostles, on the mountain of Transfiguration.

Jesus, in the throes of death, soothed the anguish of the tortured robber, by telling him that, that day, he should be with Him in Paradise.

What a solemn mockery, if the companions on the crosses were not to know, and be brought into contact with, each other in Hades!

If we believe the statements of our Bible, we cannot doubt that we shall recognize, in the Intermediate-life, those whom we have known in the Earth-life.

The yearnings of our nature ask that it *may be* so; the necessity of our being requires that it *should be* so; while the utterance of God's Word proclaims that it *is* so.

The bearing of this Deduction upon our Christian thought and experience.

It mitigates the pain which attends separation, by Death, from those we love.

That is an experience which every one of us has to face, and it is probably of all experiences the most bitter.

Consider it a moment. You, we will suppose, are a warm-hearted, affectionate man, sufficiently like Christ to want some one, be she mother, sister, or wife upon whom you may lavish your love. God gives you a wife, and as the years roll on, the interests, experiences, hopes, joys and sorrows of both become so interwoven that you "twain are one flesh." But Death comes, and with it separation. Henceforward, the bond which linked you together exists, you think, only as a memory; and an awful blight of bereavement and disappointment settles upon your future.

Or, it may be, you are a gentle, self-denying mother, and for the child whom God has given you, you would sacrifice your life if occasion required. But he dies, and a saddened, far-away look in the eyes tells that the music of your life has resolved itself into the minor key. You hold the Christian

faith, as it is commonly taught, but it is shadowy
and indefinite, and does not illumine the dark gulf
of separation between you and your boy. You
would be hurt were any one to question your belief
in a Hereafter for the child and yourself. But somehow or other the belief does not remove the feeling that you have *lost* your child.

Such is a common enough experience, but a very
dreadful one.

But what if you import into that experience the
truth concerning an Intermediate-life! What if you
believe, as you stand in the death-chamber, that the
white, coffined form is no more your wife, or child,
than the dress or coat which hangs disused in the
wardrobe! What if you can realize that they are
living, that instant, as really as you yourself are,
and that when your time to leave the Earth-life
shall come, you and they shall meet and talk, love
and be together, as in days past!

When transfigured with such thoughts, what a
very different aspect does separation bear. What
an element of grief-assuaging expectation is infused
into our sorrow for the departed when we are con-

vinced that the relationships of the Earth-life, except those into which the carnal element enters, will be renewed in the Hades-life.

The mother who on earth taught her little one to say its prayers, will, I believe, in the Intermediate-life be the one who will teach the same little one more and more of God and truth.

The friend of the Earth-life who has influenced us for good, depend upon it, will be the one, in the Hades-life, who will be used by God to woo us on to higher spiritual attainments. The beloved parent, parted from our sight for years, will be the one to greet us as we step over the threshold of the Unseen World.

Nor can I account such deeply-cherished longings the outcome of fancy.

In the course of my duty, I was ministering at the death-bed of a young woman. She was dying of consumption in a London Hospital, and was perfectly conscious to the last. Immediately before she passed away, she called, by name, a sister who had died two years previously. Then, opening wide her eyes, which had a look in them which it

was impossible to mistake—a look of recognition,—
she said as a smile passed over her thin, wasted
face, "I am coming, Annie, dear." The next instant she was gone. My own belief is that that
girl passed into the next Life in company with
a sister whom she recognized, and who had been
permitted to come to her at the moment of
transition.

Why should it be thought incredible that this was
the case? We, as Christians, profess to believe the
Bible, and in it are recorded instances of the departed having reappeared on earth, and yet when
we are confronted with testimony, borne by those
as truth-loving as ourselves, regarding like appearances, we shake our heads and pronounce it an impossibility, or a delusion. Why should it be either
the one or the other? If it be an impossibility, then
departed Samuel and Moses were *not* seen by those
living on this earth when they revisited it after
death, and consequently, no reliability can be placed
on the utterances of Scripture.

If it be a delusion, then it is so ingrained in human
experience, that mankind of every condition, clime

and age has been under it, while an inspired Apostle himself fell a victim to it.

I will not assert that all accounts of appearances after death, current in all quarters of the globe, and extending as far back as human history reaches, are truthful in every case and in all particulars. It has ever been man's part, whether in religion or anything else, to encrust truth with error and exaggeration. But I do say that it would have been impossible for there to be this world-wide testimony as to these appearances, if there had been no substratum of truth in it.

That truth is, that, in numerous well-attested instances, the departed have been seen and recognized by those still remaining in the Earth-life. And thus another reason is afforded us for believing that our contact with them in the Hades-life will embrace recognition.

We Christians, for the most part, have invested death with such surroundings as, practically, to give the lie to our faith. The hideous paraphernalia of woe; the pagan symbolism which lurks under our burial customs; the disfigurement of our tombs and gravestones with the representation of skulls and crossbones; our habit of speaking and thinking of a departed one as if non-existent—what is all this but a potent hindrance to the realization of the fact of the Intermediate-life.

For the credit of our religion, let it be said that we are slowly advancing to a better perception of truth. But to the minds of many, the mists of uncertainty and vagueness hang thickly about "the valley of the shadow of death." I have lost for a while by death many near and dear to me, and before I had grasped this grand truth of the Hades-life, I thought of them as *dead*.

Twenty-two years ago, the first—a sister of seventeen—departed. I was wont every Sunday afternoon to visit her grave. To me she seemed to be lying there. I felt that, beside that mound, I was near a *dead* loved one.

God has taught me much since then. I think of her, now, not as a lifeless form awful in the dissolution of death, but as a *living* being, as conscious as I am; in company with a beloved father and others who have since joined her in that Unseen World. To me, neither she, nor they, are dead.

Many years later, I stood beside the death-bed of another sister, and saw her, with unclouded mind, under most terrible physical suffering, calmly look into the face of death without a shudder or a fear. Almost her last words were to promise that she would always pray for us, and would give our love to that separated father and others whom she was joining, and would tell them that I never forget them in my prayers.

Is any reader of these words shocked at the mention of "prayers for the dead"? They are not prayers for the dead, but prayers for the *living;* for has not Jesus said, "all *live* unto God"? Does not Christ's religion teach us to pray for one another, and can there be found one passage in God's Word which says that we must *not* pray for our dear ones, when once they have been separated from us?

What an inexpressible sadness there is in the false idea that it is wrong to utter such prayers.

Up to the moment of death we may plead ever so earnestly with our Heavenly Father for a dear one:

an instant later, we must not. What an inconsistency, when we profess to believe that that one is
still living, and has but changed his locality!

On the other hand, what an immeasurable conso-
lation and mitigation of the pang of separation is it,
if we think our prayers may go with, and follow
him into the Intermediate-life!

I know of nothing which will make that Life so
much a reality to us, and which will bring home to
our mind the truth that there will be reunion and
recognition there, as this remembrance of the departed at the throne of grace. Instead of the bond
which has hitherto existed between us and them
being rudely snapped asunder by death, such prayer
does but strengthen it, by associating it the more
closely with God. And instead of the former love
and sympathy between us resolving themselves into
fading memories connected with a receding past,
both are preserved, and gather intensity as the time
of reunion approaches.

Thus, prayer for the departed keeps alive our
faith in the truth of recognition and reunion in the
Unseen World; while that truth bridges, as nothing

else can do, the terrible gulf of separation; and so such prayer becomes one of the grandest of influences for diverting our gaze from "things temporal," and fixing it upon "things eternal."

DEDUCTION III.

That there are different spheres of experience in the Hades-life.

Here again, the statements of the Bible, not less than the dictates of reason, compel us to differ *in toto* from the popular, but crude, conception entertained.

The prevalent idea is that when a person in a state of salvation crosses the frontier of Earth-life, and steps into the Hades-life, he is introduced at once into a place or condition, where all differences and distinctions will be for ever obliterated.

Two men, both of them Christians, in the Earth-life, may be altogether dissimilar in character and spiritual attainments; yet it is supposed by many that this dissimilarity will vanish as soon as they enter the next World.

In the latter, according to the teaching of some,

there will be no diversity either in character or surroundings. Uniformity will prevail throughout.
All will be equally circumstanced; all, in character
and attainments, counterparts one of another; and
all, to exactly the same degree, saved and possessed
of an immediately-acquired moral and spiritual perfection. The repentant and believing prize-fighter
and wife-murderer, we are told, will step from the
scaffold into the blissful condition and locality occupied by St. John and St. Paul; and this, the instant
he enters the Intermediate-life.

The only supposition under which it would be
possible to conceive of this being the case, is that
the *act of dying* works a moral miracle.

If the gasping out of one's last breath be invested
with such potency as to instantaneously transform
a sinner into a saint; a man with no character, into
a being endowed with every grace, then, we might
conceive of uniformity of life and experience in the
Hades-life.   But not otherwise.

The fact is, God's moral miracles are wrought not
in the act of dying; but in the act of *living*.   Moral
perfection is no more reached at a single bound

than is physical and intellectual perfection. No mere change of locality will effect it.

But although human existence in the Hades-World, will present differences in characters and experiences, there are certain Earth-life dissimilarities which will disappear.

The unlikeness between men, arising from the *adventitious* circumstances of Earth-life, will cease to exist in the Intermediate-life. In this world, one man may exhibit mental culture and refinement in taste; while the mind of another may be undeveloped, and his habits boorish. And when we come to trace the cause of this difference, it may be found to hinge upon a mere question of money.

The dissimilarity between the two men would, probably, not have existed, at least, not to the same extent, if the fathers of both had been so pecuniarily circumstanced as to have been able to afford to their son the like advantages of education.

Thus the adventitious circumstance of being possessed of a few hundred pounds may be the determining cause whereby one man, in this life, moves in a different intellectual and social sphere from that of another man.

But, in the Intermediate-life it will not be so. Whatever differences may there exist, this element of causation, certainly, will not.

When a man steps into that Life, the veneer of worldly position will peel off from him. Dives will leave behind him his "purple and fine linen," as Lazarus, his poverty and rags. The man who is descended from an earl, and has lived in a palace, will not, on that account, be assigned a sphere marked off from that which will be occupied by a blacksmith's son who may have dwelt in a cottage. The differences which exist there, are *moral* differences, arising from variety in *character and spiritual attainment.*

There is such a thing as a "*babe* in Christ," and a "*man* in Christ." If one enters that Life as a "babe" in character and spiritual attainment, he must not expect that his lot, so long as he remains a "babe," will be cast among "spirits made perfect." There would be as much unfitness in it, as there would be in transplanting a child from an In-

fant-school into a University, or in apportioning to
a boy the environment of a man. St. Paul, as we
have seen, was permitted an experience of the Intermediate-life of a very exalted kind, and he is very
careful to describe his condition, at the time, as
that of a "*man* in Christ" (2 Cor. xii. 2). Had he
been a "babe" when that experience was vouchsafed to him, his being "caught up into Paradise,"
would not have involved his entrance into "the
third heaven," or sphere, of it.

Let us examine more closely this truth, as to there
being different spheres of experience and life in
Hades.

There is certainly a great difference between the
experience and life of those who enter that World
in a state of salvation, and those who do not. By
a "state of salvation," I mean what our Church
means, when she uses in her Catechism the same
expression. It does not imply that the character
has been moulded, and the spiritual nature developed. It simply denotes that a person is on the
right road to that end. He may have advanced only
a few steps along that road, or he may have accom-

plished the half, or even the greater part of the distance. But, whatever may be the stage he has reached, he is in a "state of salvation."

If, in leaving the Earth-life, and passing into the Hades-life, one man be in that "state," and another be not, the sphere of continued existence will be different. The parable of the rich man and Lazarus teaches this. The existence of both men is therein depicted as it was immediately after death.

Both, according to the Greek, had passed into Hades; but not into the same sphere. Their experiences were widely dissimilar. The beggar's was one of relief and happiness; the unfeeling, rich man's, that of self-reproach and unhappiness.

Moreover, to emphasize this fact of difference in sphere, our Lord represents Abraham as saying, that between Lazarus and Dives "is a great gulf fixed"—a gulf formed by dissimilarity in taste, desire, and character, between one loving God, and another not loving Him; between one whose moral and spiritual instincts are developing, and another in whom those instincts are wanting. That this gulf is not everlastingly fixed, but only as long as

the dissimilarity exists, is shown by the fact
that although our Lord at death passed into
Paradise, yet He went and preached "the Gospel"
to the Antediluvians—a class of notorious sinners,
who at death had been alienated from God and
goodness.

Nor need we think it strange that there should be
this gulf. It exists in this Earth-life, although not
so sharply defined. It yawns between the Christian and the unbeliever. In the noblest part of their
being—their sympathies and aspirations—they are
separated.

Sharers though they may be in the same external
circumstances of life, there is, nevertheless, an
inner domain of thought in which the Self of each
is dwelling apart from the other.

It is so in the Hades-life, only with this difference, that when the extraneous surroundings of
Earth-life shall have disappeared, the moral and
spiritual distinction will be the more apparent.

Again, there are different spheres of experience
and life, in the case of those entering Hades *in a
"state of salvation."*

There are some who pass into that Life, mellowed and ripened, after sixty or seventy years of training by God the Holy Ghost. There are others who in middle-life have turned to Christ, and within a year or two afterwards, enter it. Many have disregarded religion until the hair has become whitened, and then, within a few months of their change, depart thither. And a few do not seek the Saviour until the sands of life are on the point of running out.

The whole of an octogenarian Earth-life is not too long for the formation of the Christ-life character, and the development of the spiritual nature; and yet millions of Christians die before reaching the age of thirty.

What are we to imagine concerning these ? That the same sphere of life and experience will be equally suitable to all ? Assuredly not. Some, at the moment of translation, have but planted their feet on the lowest rungs of the ladder, whose top is perfection. Others have ascended many rungs. Some are half-way up; while a comparative few are within a measurable distance of the top. Will there be no difference in the attitude of the one who is at the bottom of the ladder, and that of the man who has all but reached the top? The higher the ascent, the more comprehensive the range of vision. A man with an unformed character and an undeveloped spiritual nature, would be as out of place and uncomfortable in the "*third heaven*" of Paradise, as a barn-door fowl translated to a lofty crag of the Alps, or as the blind fish in the cave of Kentucky were they suddenly located in the ocean. An adaptation to environment would be wanting.

Just as, in the physical universe, beings find their lot cast in a sphere suitable to their capacities, and can only rise to higher spheres of existence by a corresponding enlargement of capacities, so is it in the Intermediate-life. In the new experience into which we enter at death, we gravitate to a sphere, for which, by the character we have formed during the Earth-life, we have adapted ourselves. Our position there will answer exactly to the degree of sanctification which has been wrought in us by the Holy Ghost, in the period before death. The road to the distant goal of moral and spiritual perfection is a long one, and every inch of the way must be

traversed. When death overtakes those who, for
many years, have been patiently and perseveringly
plodding along that road, they will find themselves,
in the Unseen-life, within a measurable distance of
the end. On the other hand, when death comes to
those who have but only just commenced the jour-
ney, the goal will be far ahead. And between the
starters and the finishers will be an intervening distance.

The bearing of this Deduction upon our Christian thought and experience.

*It will impress upon us, as no other consideration
will, the vast importance of cultivating, in* THIS LIFE,
our character and spirit. It will lead us Christians
to do what St. Paul, with his knowledge of the Intermediate-life, urged that we should do—"work
out our own salvation with fear and trembling." It
will be impossible with this truth in view to be
careless as to the cultivation of character. Knowing the intimate connection which exists between
our character here, and our experiences hereafter,
we shall not live slipshod Christian lives, in the
hope that, somehow or another, all will come right

at the moment of death. And yet thousands, who are not insensible to Christ's Gospel, are so living. Why is it that so many Christians never seem to grow in grace? Why is there so little effort to rid themselves of defects in character? Why, after thirty years of Christian instruction, do they appear no nearer moral perfection? How comes it that there are such beings as "*unlovely*" Christians, who in spite of their church-going and orthodoxy, are cold, unsympathetic, selfish, or cross-tempered?

Is it not that, intermingled with their belief, there is an idea that, after all, the cultivation of character, during the Earth-life, is not a matter of paramount concern; that so long as certain doctrines be held, and certain religious ordinances observed, all will be right at the last; that as soon as they step out of this world, there will be a wonderful moral-transformation, and in an instant, apart from any effort of theirs, they will become all that they sincerely desire to become?

Thousands of Christian people are positively indifferent about the formation of character, because they do not realize that God means what He says, when He states, that "whatsoever a man soweth, *that* shall he also reap."

Take, for a moment, this particular passage.

What, let me ask, is the interpretation put upon it by nine out of every ten persons? I venture to say that it has been so explained by a number of theologians, as to mean the *exact opposite* of what it asserts.

I will instance the case of a man, to whom, inasmuch as he accepts and believes the doctrines of Christianity, the term "Christian" cannot be denied. But he has never grasped the truth concerning existence in the Intermediate-life, and as a consequence, he has been careless about the development of character. He knows that a dying robber, even after a life of indifference and wickedness, turned to a pitiful Saviour, and was saved. However faulty he may be, he is not so bad as that man was, and he hopes and believes that his moral crookedness will be made straight, and the cavities of character filled in, *some day*. Press him for an answer to the question as to *when* this will happen, and he will reply that he supposes it will be *when he dies.* Why he should think so, he does not know; he cannot adduce a single passage of Scripture to warrant the assumption; he only supposes it will be so.

But all the time, he is overlooking a most important consideration, which is, that his neglect of character constitutes a moral seed-sowing, in regard to which the reaping in another Life will correspond. The thought may be distasteful, but he can no more get away from the fact, than he can ignore the parallel law which obtains in the physical universe, viz., that weed-seeds produce weeds, and corn-seeds, corn.

Because he has been unconcerned, or but little concerned, in regard to character, he may have acquired traits of selfishness and want of sympathy. Around his manner may have grown up a brusqueness, or unattractiveness. Bad-temper, irritability, peevishness, indolence, or untruthfulness may have been unchecked in his moral system.

This will have been a seed-sowing, and with regard to that, God has said, "Whatsoever a man soweth, *that* shall he also reap." The man, at last, dies; repentant for his sins; really sorry that he is not better; and with a sincere faith in Christ as his Saviour.

What then ? Will such an one reap *as* he had sown ? Ask the majority of Christian teachers. Will not this be the sort of answer you will elicit ? "Well, no: you see that man died in the Christian faith. His sins have been pardoned, and the imperfections, cavities, and want of development in his character and spiritual nature all disappeared at the moment of death. *As a believer*, he will *not* reap as he had sown. Had he been an *unbeliever*, of course, he would have done so."

And in this way, the statement of Scripture that one will reap *as*, *i. e.*, *according as* he has sown, is flatly contradicted. It is made to be an untruth with regard to some persons. It is a fact in the case of unbelievers; it is *not* so in that of believers.

But I take exception to this kind of teaching, and say, that we cannot so juggle with God's eternal laws. They are universal in their application. This particular law of correspondence between sowing

and reaping is as true of Christians as of those who
are not Christians.   There is not an indication in
the Bible which warrants us in supposing that, in
any instance, it will be inoperative.   We shall reap,
in the Intermediate-life, as we have sown in the
Earth-life.   The character we have shaped, and the
spiritual advancement we have made here will correspond to the position which we shall occupy
there.   Those of us who are neglecting the formation of character may possibly enter the Hades-life
in "a state of salvation"; because no one who
turns to Christ, even at the eleventh hour, can remain lost; but the consequence of a past neglect
will be experienced.   Instead of passing into the
"*third heaven*" of Paradise, an unformed character
and undeveloped nature may require that we sub-
mit ourselves to the discipline and ordeal of a *lower*
school.

If we be wise men, the truth that there are different spheres of experience in the Hades-World, will
goad us into being earnest about our life and character.   Just as we dare not be neglectful of our education in youth, because our position in later years

will be affected thereby; so the cultivation of our moral and spiritual nature will be a task to which we shall devote ourselves, for the reason that we shall know that the neglect of it may involve a handicapping of ourselves in the Life to come.

Thus, human existence will assume a greater responsibility and significance; new incentive will be given to the struggle after holiness; and a greater importance will attach itself to even the thoughts, looks, and words, as well as the actions, of our every-day life.

Then, our chief concern will be so to live, that when "the garish lights" of Earth shall wax dim, and go out, we may enter into such a sphere of the Unseen-life as to pass easily on unto perfection.

DEDUCTION IV.

That a work of perfecting and developing will go on in the Hades-life.

This Deduction arises naturally out of the preceding one, and is closely associated with it.

If, as we have seen, there are different spheres of

life and experience in Hades, those spheres will be occupied by persons exhibiting various degrees of attainment. The character and spiritual nature of some will be inferior to that of others. Some will be nearer perfection than others. And yet both classes may consist of those who are in "a state of salvation."

But their being in "a state of salvation" involves their identification with a scheme which is pledged to accomplish in them a *perfecting*, bodily, morally and spiritually.

That is the work to which the Gospel stands committed. It is no mere device for rescuing men from Hell and the "Second Death"; but a magnificent provision whereby they can be remodelled into moral images of God.

Now, unless the Gospel is to fail in its purpose, one of three things must happen. Either the moral and spiritual perfecting of a Christian must take place *before death;* in *the act of dying;* or *in the Intermediate-life.* It cannot take place in the existence subsequent to this latter, *i. e.*, the Heaven or Celestial-life because that condition starts with

perfection as an accomplished fact. We shall
begin the Heaven-life with a Resurrection-body.
Throughout the New Testament, the Resurrection
condition is viewed, as being the Goal, or Consummation of Christ's Redemption. It will be the
crowning act of a long continued work of perfecting. Inasmuch as there would be an incompatibility
in associating, in the Heaven-life, a perfect body
with an imperfect spirit, it follows that the occu-
pant of the "heavenly-house" will be suitable for
that house. In other words, the being of resurrection and life who will enter Heaven, will be a being
from whose character and spirit every vestige of
imperfection will have been eliminated. Our
Lord's words surely teach this—"No man putteth a
piece of *new* cloth unto an *old* garment."

When, then, is this perfecting of the spirit accomplished? Certainly, not entirely *before* death.
However grand and beautiful the character of one
may be at the close of a long Christian life, there
are yet flaws and cavities in his nature which mark
him as still being imperfect. If any be disposed to
challenge this assertion, I would ask, how, other-

wise, is it that many exemplary Christians, on their death-bed, have exhibited temper or selfishness?

Assuredly, it will not be accomplished *in the act of dying*, unless we do violence to our common sense, and upset all we know with regard to God's physical and spiritual laws. There is no more reason for thinking that the work of perfecting can be brought about suddenly by the disrupting hand of Death, than there is for supposing that the cracking of the shell will make the newly-hatched chick a full-grown fowl. To state that a repentant murderer, the moment after execution, will have a character devoid of fault, and a spirit replete with grace, is as contrary to sense, as in saying that an infant immediately after birth is in possession of all the developments of manhood.

The work of bringing a human spirit to a state of full development and perfection, is infinitely greater than bringing anything in the physical universe to the same relative condition. And yet, in respect to physical things, nothing reaches perfection except by slow stages of growth and advancement. Are we to imagine that the *greater* work will be more easily achieved; that, while ages are required for the formation of the earth's crust, and years, for the growth of an oak-tree, the moments occupied in gasping out one's last breath, will suffice for the modelling of an unshaped character? It is no wonder that a theology which has taught this has failed to commend itself to scientific thought.

Seeing, then, that the perfecting of the spirit, in the majority of instances (at all events), is not accomplished *before* Death, and certainly, is not, in *the act of dying*, we are shut up to the conclusion that *this work will go on in the Intermediate-life.*

Before I proceed further with the discussion of this Deduction, let me say that I repudiate the doctrine of "Purgatory," as taught by the Roman Catholic Church. That doctrine, in my judgment, is materialistic, revolting, childish, and calculated to do immeasurable harm. History has shown that it has been a powerful instrument in the hands of an unscrupulous priesthood for striking terror into the minds of an unenlightened and too credulous laity. It has, in the past, even caused religion to degenerate into a scheme of money-making.

But at the same time, it is too often forgotten that the grotesque doctrine has been built up upon a grand and sublime truth. The *foundation* is scriptural and good; but upon that foundation human teachers have reared a superstructure of rubbish. If it were not so—if there had been no foundation of truth—the doctrine of Purgatory would long since have ceased to be believed. There are thoughtful men, to-day, who do believe it, though not, perhaps, in its coarse, Mediæval representation; and how it becomes possible for them to do so, is, that underlying a very great amount of error is the truth, that, in the Hades-life, there is a work of perfecting and developing.

If the word "Purgatory" be used only to denote a "purging out" of sin and imperfection, I know of nothing objectionable in it. Our Church of England has not a word to say against it. What she condemns, in her 22d Article, is the "*Romish doctrine* concerning Purgatory."

Two very weighty considerations render the fact of there being a perfecting and development in the Hades-life a *necessity*. One is: that it harmonizes

with what we know to be God's method of pro-
ceeding in the work of salvation.   The other is, that
it alone answers objections which can be urged
against the *fair-dealing* of God.

Take the first consideration.   What do we know
in regard to the Almighty's work of saving men?
Precisely what we know in respect to every other
work of His, viz., that all has been done under, and
in obedience to, His universal law of growth and
development.   That law obtains equally in the
realm of spirit as in the world of matter.   It has
characterized the scheme of redemption throughout.   Part of that scheme consists in revealing to
mankind the central truth of the Gospel—the incarnation of God the Son, and His sacrifice for the salvation of the world.   Another part consists in destroying "the works of the devil."   While a third,
is to make man what he was intended to be—an
image of God.

Now, it is quite clear that the work involved in
the first two parts of this scheme has come under
the great law of progression.

The truth of the Incarnation and Atonement was

very slowly and very gradually made known to men.

Age after age of Levitical prefigurement and prophetical foreshadowing passed away before mankind knew the truth as we know it; and in our own times, the knowledge is being but slowly diffused; while the day seems yet distant when "the earth shall be filled with it, as the waters cover the sea" (Hab. ii. 14).

Then, again, the task of destroying "the works of the devil" is *a very slow one.* The preaching of Christianity, for eighteen hundred years, has had an enormous influence for good on society. The world of to-day is vastly better than it was in the times of ancient Greece and Rome. But still the reign of evil is far from being at an end.

We come to the third part of the Gospel scheme, which is to make man an image of God, and we are asked by some to believe that the law of gradual growth and development which is so plainly seen to be an underlying principle in the working out of the first two parts is laid aside in this. To put it in another way. In working out parts 1 and 2 of the

Gospel scheme, God acts consistently with an universal law; while in working out part 3, He does not. This is no over-statement of the case. At eight o'clock a condemned felon, who in view of death has repented, is a wretched sinner with an unshapen character, an undeveloped mind, and any amount of evil tendencies. At five minutes past eight, the hangman's rope has launched him into the Intermediate-life, and, according to some, the work of salvation has been accomplished; with the exception of the crowning act, viz., that he will one day obtain a resurrection body. He may have been a Christian for less than one hour, but that does not prevent him from being transformed into a saint the instant he is removed from the Earth-life.

Those who teach such doctrine will admit that the formation of their own and other Christians' character is a very gradual work; that fifty or sixty years of Divine training is not too much to bring a man within a measurable distance of perfection. And yet they find no difficulty in believing, as regards some, that a work so transcendently hard can

be effected in a few moments. Of course, we shall
be told that the intervention of Death makes all the
difference. But what is this but mistaking the
power which Death is capable of wielding. The
domain of this Death is in the material and not in
the spiritual. It can touch only the bodies of men;
it cannot affect their spirits. A thousand deaths
would never raise the soul who survived them
one hair's breadth nearer moral or spiritual perfection.

But an escape from this difficulty is sometimes
sought by saying that Death itself does not work
this change in the spirit, but God does. It is said,
"Would you limit the omnipotence of the Almighty? Is He not able to effect in an *instant*
what, ordinarily, He only effects slowly and gradually?" My answer to this is, that it is not a question of what God is *able* to do, but what He
actually does.

He *could* have revealed to mankind in a moment
a Gospel which He took ages to unfold. He *could*
have destroyed "the works of the devil" by one
annihilating blow of His sledge-hammer of omnipo-

tence. He *could* have stifled every impulse to evil, and have caused every grace to start forth in full bloom within us, at our first cry for pardon.

But we are confronted with the fact that He has *not done* so, and to assert that He will lay aside His universal law and proceed on other lines, needs the very strongest testimony of Scripture to make it believable.

That testimony is not forthcoming. There is not one passage in the Bible which states, or even implies, that the work of perfecting can be effected suddenly, or completed at the moment of death. Such passages as " Let us *go on* unto perfection" (Heb. vi. 1), " *Patient continuance* in well doing" (Rom. ii. 7), " Till we all come . . . unto a perfect man" (Eph. iv. 13), " The *spirits* of just men *made perfect*" (Heb. xii. 23), " He which hath begun a good work in you will perform it until the day of Jesus Christ" (Phil. i. 6), and a number of other like passages imply prolonged effort, and are fatal to the conception that the work of perfecting can be achieved easily or suddenly. They are in agreement with all that the Bible tells us of God's moral workings, and with all that science proclaims regarding His physical operations, viz, that "the God of patience" (Rom. xv. 5) does nothing spasmodically.

If, then, there be some who leave the Earth-life before ever the work of perfecting be commenced, as in the case of death-bed repentances; if there be others who die at an *early* age—and millions of Christians do so; and if, moreover, there be those who, after a long life, are yet faulty in character and undeveloped in spirit, God's great law of growth and progression makes it a *necessity* that there should be a perfecting and developing in the Hades-life. And this particular phase of the work of Salvation is in harmony with all the other phases of it. There is uniformity throughout.

Glance now at the other consideration which makes a perfecting and developing in the Hades-life a *necessity*. I mean that which affects the question of *fair-dealing* on the part of God.

Now I am aware that, by some, it is supposed to be a sort of Christian duty to scare one off this ground by hinting that the discussion of God's *fair-*

dealing savors of presumption. One may talk as much as one likes about His omnipotence and holiness, but this particular attribute of the Deity must not be subjected to enquiry.

If a crude presentiment of Divine truth makes it difficult for us to see how this quality can be ascribed to God, the answer is always at hand,— " My thoughts are not your thoughts, neither are your ways My ways, saith the Lord " (Is. lx. 8).

But why, when this passage is quoted, is the context so persistently kept out of sight ? The prophet tells us that God's ways are "*higher*" than our ways, and His thoughts than our thoughts. Divine qualities have been so pared away by some theologians, as not only to make them lower than the corresponding qualities in ourselves, but to destroy all resemblance to them. It is manifestly absurd to mean one thing by a certain word when applied to one person, and something different when referred to another. Fair-dealing on the part of the Almighty will be the same *in kind* as fair-dealing on our part; only it will be *greater* in quality and quantity.

I contend that a consideration of this quality of
fair-dealing, which we ascribe to God, makes it
necessary that a place be given to the work of perfecting in the Hades-life.

What is the state of things with which we are
confronted?   That hundreds of thousands of Christians are removed from the Earth *before* the work
of perfecting and development has been effected?
If that work can only be accomplished *prior* to the
moment of death, have they been dealt with fairly?
If our position be disputed, viz., that there is growth
and advancement in the Intermediate-life, then an
early death will place them at a disadvantage for all
eternity.   Is it fair that to one man should be
granted a long life to prepare for that eternity,
while another's career should be closed almost as
soon as the work has commenced? If the Earth-
life be the *only* "School," how unjust to give one
son a fifty years' training, and another son one.

And yet we are shut up to this conclusion, unless
our Fourth Deduction be admitted.

**The bearing of this Deduction upon our Chris-
tian thought and experience.**

It imparts a reasonableness to our faith, and invests the Intermediate-life with increased interest.

Take the first, that it imparts a reasonableness to our faith.

What is faith ? Not an unthinking prostration of the mind before a code of theology, however venerable with age, or stamped with ecclesiastical authority. Not an unquestioning acquiescence in certain doctrines which may have passed muster as Divine truth, a few centuries ago; nor the mere association of one's self with "orthodox" Christianity.

All this may exist, and yet produce in a person nothing more than *credulity*.

Faith is man's grasp of God and truth *with his whole moral nature*. A certain divinely-implanted instinct in man, called by Plato "the something divine" (θεῖόν τι), finds its correspondence in God and truth. In other words, the inner consciousness of man perceives, and does homage to, certain moral qualities, *e. g.*, love, mercy and fair-dealing. When God is viewed as possessing those qualities in a preeminent degree, there is established between man and his Maker a relationship which rises above the domain of the intellectual and emotional, into that of the *moral*. The moral excellence of God appealing to a moral sense in man, lifts man out of the lower sphere of religious belief, into the higher domain of *faith*. Faith is impossible, unless we are able to believe that there exists in God the ideal of those moral qualities of which we have the perception in ourselves. Denude God of these attributes, and there can be no real moral grasp of Him.

And this applies to teaching concerning God. Invest theology with characteristics which are in harmony with our own intuitions of what is moral and good, and at once an affinity is established between it and man's better nature. Shock the moral sensibilities by divesting theology of it, and religion, however earnest, will never rise above *credulity*. The hold on doctrine will be a matter of the brain, not of the moral nature; and as such it will fall short of *faith*.

We are astonished, sometimes, that what has passed currency for *faith*, should have been associated with so much that horrifies the mind of a right-thinking man. The Irish peasant will be punctilious in his attendance at Mass and Confession, but be none the less disposed to take part in a free-fight. The Romish Inquisitor subscribed most loyally to the Articles of His Church, but was ready, in the name of God, to inflict the most devilish torture upon a fellow-creature. The Calvinist divine wrote volumes in defence of Christianity, and yet attributed such conduct to the God of Love as outrages every sense of mercy and fair-dealing.

How are we to account for this? In no other way than that these persons' conceptions of the Almighty were those in which the moral instincts play little or no part.

Where there has been on the part of theologians and the adherents to Christianity, a putting into the background of God's moral qualities of justice and fair-dealing, religion has before now degenerated, both in theory and practice, into a system disfigured by consummate selfishness and revolting heartlessness.

I venture to say that God has been preached as

acting in a way toward His creatures, which is infinitely worse than anything ever ascribed to the
vilest pagan deity; while deeds have been done in
the name of Christianity which make us shudder as
we read of them.   Would you know how it was
possible that men exhibiting, in many instances,
characters noble and good, could, nevertheless,
teach that "there are infants in hell a span long,"
and that the Almighty creates the great bulk of the
human race for the express purpose of consigning
it to eternal torment?   Do you wonder how both
Romanists and Protestants could have had the heart
to torture and burn their fellow-men and women?

The answer is at hand.   They failed to justly
estimate the moral qualities of God.   The men who
taught and did these things were holders of creeds;
but the creeds were such as forbade the moral
instinct in man finding its correspondence in God.
To them, the Deity was an Almighty Despot from
whose constitution the attributes of justice and fair-
dealing had been eliminated   A distorted conception of the Divine Sovereignty caused God's moral
qualities, upon which alone that Sovereignty sub-

sists, to disappear. Is it any wonder that, when
the eternal principles of justice and fair-dealing
have been denied with respect to God, men should
refuse to do homage to the mere thought of His
Sovereignty! Tell me that God is Almighty, and
link with His Almightiness the qualities of mercy
and justice, and I can love Him. Strip His omnipotence of these qualities, and you will excite in my
breast no more than a feeling of slavish fear. The
creed of the Christian, in that case, will rest on the
same foundation as the belief of the pagan.

But when our conception of God and Divine
truth is such as to make it unnecessary to put any
one of His moral perfections into the background;
when we can think of Him as *altogether* good,
without making a reservation in regard to one or
more of His qualities; when, moreover, our code of
theology is sufficiently comprehensive to admit of
our thinking of Him without doing violence to our
own moral instincts and sensibilities, then, and only
then, will creed be invested with that reasonableness, which, commanding the allegiance of our
moral nature, will lift us into the domain of real faith.

If a perfecting and developing of the spirit of man in the Intermediate-life be denied, we have no alternative but to drop out of our religious belief the thought of God's fair-dealing and justice. On the other hand, let it be admitted, and no dispensations of His Providence, howsoever mysterious, will ever crush our conviction that these two eternal principles of goodness are resident in Him.

Thus, one important bearing of our Fourth Deduction will be to impart to Christian doctrine a credibility and reasonableness begotten of moral sanction.

We turn, now, to another consideration—the value of this Deduction *as investing the Intermediate-life with increased interest.*

It is astounding how small a place the subject of the After-life occupies in the mind of Christians generally It rarely forms the theme of the preacher; still less rarely, a topic of conversation in private life among even sincerely religious persons. A question of ecclesiastical antiquity, or of the minutiæ of ritual, is capable of evoking the liveliest interest; while this subject, so transcendently important, excites but languid attention. Why is this? Is there want of belief in this Intermediate existence between Death and the Resurrection? That can hardly be the case, seeing that every Churchman, at all events, professes to accept the Apostles' Creed wherein this truth is enshrined.

The fact is, the current conception of the Inter-mediate-life is a depressingly vague one. Many suppose that it is impossible for us on earth to know anything of that Life beyond the bare fact that it exists. Some will go farther, and say that because God in His Word has but revealed the *broad principles* which underlie existence there, it is wrong to seek for any clearly defined ideas on the subject. Let one do, as we have done, make fair and honest deductions from the statements of Scripture as to what the environment of that Life is, and he will be fortunate if he escape the charge of teaching Popery, or of drawing upon his imagination.

But it is inconsistent for us, as Churchmen, to object against fair and honest deduction as a means whereby we may arrive at a better perception of truth, seeing that several of the doctrines which we hold most tenaciously—*e. g.*, that of the Trinity and Infant Baptism—have become Articles of our creed by this means.

The result of this vagueness concerning the Inter-mediate-life; this listless acquiescence in the idea that nothing can be known about it, has been most disastrous to Christian thought and aspiration.

The Unseen-life has been robbed of its interest, and in some cases clothed with associations which are positively distasteful to many minds. Who among us does not shudder at the thought of enter-ing a world which has so often been represented as containing nothing akin to that of which we have any experience here! Take away from our concep-tion of that Life the thought that there will be re-newed intercommunion, opportunities of ministra-tion, and scope for the exercise of such qualities as affection and sympathy, and who would care for such an experience! Make it a sphere, as it has been too often depicted, where no work for God or man is done; where there is no training of the mind to higher knowledge, and the spirit to loftier gracefulness; where intelligent beings, capable of infinite activity, are to loll away an indefinite period in indolent expectation of a blessedness to come upon them, and what man of energy would not recoil from such a lot!

On the other hand, view the Intermediate-life as a place where the incompleted work of developing and perfecting will be carried on to its consummation, and how vastly more attractive and interesting does it become! What a death-blow is dealt to the delusive idea of thousands, that it practically matters little if they are careless about the development of character in the present life, because at the moment of death, if they die in the Christian faith, all will be put right! What a powerful incentive to holiness, if only it be realized that the more earnest our strivings after goodness are here, the higher our position, the less rigorous our disciplining, and the quicker and easier our transition into the condition of "just men made perfect" will be there!

What a palliative of the sadness and disappointment in seeing a promising work of growth in grace apparently interrupted by death!

What a magnificent answer to the yearnings of one whose acquirement of spiritual graces does but make him eager to possess more, and whose mounting on the lower rungs of the ladder of knowledge does but urge him to be the more anxious to climb the higher!

Thus the truth of an existence after Death whose characteristic, as that of all other life, is growth and development, flings around that existence a halo of attractiveness.

It is so to the man of science, inasmuch as he recognizes in its constitution the same great underlying principles as he detects everywhere in nature. The Gospel becomes a believable thing to him when he can think that God's laws in the spiritual sphere are the same in kind as those in the physical world. It is so to the man of Divinely cultivated instincts, inasmuch as this truth concerning the Intermediate-life touches him in his profoundest and most tender experiences.

And it is in this last respect, that the truth we are considering bears, perhaps, most of all upon Christian thought.

We will suppose that you are one who views the cultivation of character, and the attainment of spiritual perfection, as the paramount concern of life. You view the Gospel, not as a mere contrivance whereby men can escape the consequences of wrong-doing, but as a magnificent means by which they can be restored to the moral image of God. Saturated with this thought, you give your mind to the stupendous task. You pray for Divine assistance; you set a watch upon your words and actions; you scrutinize motives and impulses: you prune away habits, pursuits, and surroundings which you consider are antagonistic to the end in view; and you foster all that is likely to advance the same. You are sincere in your religion; your belief is a reality to you. So, you go on, let us say, for twenty years. At the end of that time, something or another causes you to take spiritual stock of yourself. It may have been brought about by reading a book, or by listening to a sermon, or by coming into contact with one exhibiting a beautiful, Christlike character. Your stock-taking is a bitter disappointment to you. You discover that you are immeasurably short of what you would like to be. Many spiritual cavities are visible, and innumerable defects of character distress you. Still you pursue the task, while a more bitter disappointment awaits you.

Your health has failed: you are dying; and you know for a certainty that in a few weeks or months at most your Earth-life will have closed. As an educated man, you know, also, that it is opposed to the order of the universe, and to every known law of God, to imagine that the mere physical act of dying can achieve a moral and spiritual work which years of living have not been able to effect. Moreover, you know that this work cannot be done other than slowly and gradually.

Without the thought that that work will be continued in the Intermediate-life, what remains? Only the unavailing regret that, in eternity, you will be less than you might have been, if only the Almighty had seen fit to let you live on earth longer. Will you not loathe a Death, and hate an existence which enforces upon you such a disappointment? Will the adornment of your spirit with a Resurrection-body, however glorious, compensate for the condition of arrested development in that spirit?

But view the Unseen-life as a life of continued progress until moral and spiritual perfection be reached, and to a dying Christian man, as I have instanced, how pregnant with interest will it become! With St. Paul, he will say, as he steps into that Life, "Not as though I had already attained, either were already perfect; but I follow after" (Phil. iii. 12).

Take one other experience which comes to many. God has given you a little child. As a Christian, you are intensely anxious that that child should grow up to a manhood stamped with moral and spiritual excellence. Year after year, finds you earnest in your efforts to impart to him a knowledge of Divine truth. Tendencies to evil are checked; those to good encouraged. The tone of your boy's character is as much a concern to you as your own salvation.

Years roll on. The boy has become a lad. The future looks promising for the realization of your hopes respecting him. Already the first green blades of a harvest of noble qualities are visible in him. You thank God for it, and within a year, may be, stand heart-broken beside his coffin. "Oh! God," you cry in your anguish, "that this curtailed life should cut short my golden aspirations in respect to my boy!"

What, I ask, will yield one scrap of comfort at such a time, but the belief that the noble work commenced by you on earth, will be continued in the Unseen-life into which your child has gone! How the interest centred in that Life will be enhanced to you, if it be viewed as the "Upper-school" of your dear one! What a depth of meaning will be contained in the poet's words!

> "She is not dead,—the child of our affection,—
>   But gone unto that School,
>   Where she no longer needs our poor protection,
>   And Christ Himself doth rule.
>   Day after day, we think what she is doing,
>   In those bright realms of air;
>   Year after year, her tender steps pursuing,
>   Behold her grown more fair.
>
> "Not as a child shall we again behold her;
>   For when with raptures wild,
>   In our embraces we again enfold her,
>   She will not be a child;

> But a fair maiden, in her Father's mansion,
> Clothed with celestial grace ;
> And beautiful with all the soul's expansion
> Shall we behold her face."

Can anything, as the truth embodied in our Fourth Deduction, exert so powerful an influence upon Christian thought and experience, not only as making our Creed reasonable, but as investing the existence after Death with interest and charm!

DEDUCTION V.

That there is a preaching of Christ's Gospel in the Intermediate-life, which warrants us in believing that the work of saving mankind is extended beyond the grave.

The view which has obtained currency in the past, and which is still entertained by a large number of Christians, is, that our Lord's work of saving souls is absolutely restricted to the Earth-life; so that, when once the breath has departed from the body of a person who may not have died with a saving knowledge of the truth, his doom is fixed. No matter however unfavorable his lot in this

world may have been; however unfortunate his
environment; however small his chances compared
with those of others, according to some, it makes
no difference.   What he will be for all eternity is
determined by what he is at the moment of death.
And the irresistible logic of this merciless conception is to make Death the hurler of ninety-nine out
of·every hundred persons into a hopeless perdition.

But, surely, we have a right to expect that a
doctrine so subversive of all which we account
good, fair and merciful, ought not to command the
assent of Christians, unless it can be shown that it
is based upon plain and unequivocal statements of
Scripture.   If that can *not* be shown, then, the
Church of to-day has as much right to discard this
particular view, as any other false religious idea
which may have been held in the past.   In the
middle ages, the Roman Catholic Church taught
that it was pleasing in the sight of God to torture
and burn heretics.   Later on, the divines of our
own Church preached as part of the Gospel a hideous doctrine of Reprobation.   How many, in the
Church of England, hold either of those views, to-day?

They were in opposition to the spirit of Christ, and the Word of God, and an age of fuller knowledge and clearer enlightenment has perceived it, and discarded them.

Now, I have no hesitation in saying that there is no more foundation in Scripture for assuming that there can be no saving *after* death, than there is for the act of torturing heretics, or for teaching Reprobation. I have been challenged, again and again, by those who have differed from me as regards this Fifth Deduction, and when I have asked for the Scriptural proofs upon which an opposite opinion can be based, the following has been the only passage adduced—"In the place where the tree falleth there it shall be " (Eccles. xi. 3).

But, surely, no serious student of Divine truth will place this utterance of a backsliding man, who at times was all but engulphed in agnosticism, beside the statements of Apostles, whose minds had been specially illuminated at Pentecost. Many of the utterances in Ecclesiastes are completely opposed to the teaching of our Lord, and are recorded in the Sacred Canon merely to show

how perverted the spirit's judgment of things may become when the rein is given to lust and worldly-mindedness.

Furthermore, where is there, in the passage in question, the slightest indication that it has reference to man's *spiritual* condition at all ? Do not the verses which precede it show that the writer was referring to *temporal* surroundings, without a thought of eternity ? How absurd, then, to raise upon such a weak foundation as this a superstructure of doctrine, which has dwarfed the Gospel of Christ, by flatly contradicting hundreds of passages of Scripture, and has caused untold thousands of thoughtful men to turn shudderingly away from Christianity! We have cause to be thankful that the theology of the present day is becoming immeasurably more humane, and is losing that impress of barbaric thought which stamped itself upon the Western Church after the Apostolic age. The representation of the Almighty which passed muster for orthodoxy, in the 16th and 17th centuries, would not be tolerated to-day.

But the advance to a clearer and better perception

of Divine truth is necessarily slow.   It is very difficult to loosen the tenacious grasp of error on the
minds of men.   It is no easy thing to efface a misconception which may have grown up with us
from childhood, and still less easy to shake the idea
that the Church of God, in this age, cannot possibly
know more of truth than the Church in past ages;
although history bears witness to the contrary.

And so prejudice, and a servile prostration of the
mind before the doctrinal pronouncements of ages
less enlightened than our own, bar the way for
many to a fuller understanding of God's Word.

There is one thing which astonishes me beyond
measure, and that is, that any attempt to show
from Scripture that the salvation of Christ is more
embracive than has been commonly imagined, calls
forth a display of the bitterest hostility, and the
most cruel misrepresentation.   It is one of the
puzzles of human nature.   Unless experience had
taught us otherwise, we should be inclined to think
that a Christianity whose chief characteristic is described by St. Paul as being "charity" which
" *hopeth all things*," would hail with intense delight

the thought of salvation beyond the grave for poor unfortunates who have lived and died without, in some cases, one of the religious advantages which we enjoy. That the attitude of a man or woman, bearing the name of a pitiful Christ, toward any suggestion of such a hope would be, "Thank God! Tell me, are there any statements in the Bible upon which I can rest such a magnificent belief? How devoutly I wish you may be right in what you say! How far more glorious and attractive will it make the Gospel to me!"

But no; strange as it may be, the tendency of some minds is toward a creed of merciless severity. Preachers have earned the reputation of being able exponents of Scripture, and "Gospel" preachers, who have attributed to the God, whose name is "Love," conduct sufficient to shock the sensibilities of a Hottentot; while those who, Bible in hand, have ventured to cast a doubt upon the miserable restrictions which men have set upon Divine love and mercy, have been loaded with abuse, and branded as heretics and enemies of truth.

The dread of arousing antagonism influences the

conduct of numbers of the clergy who hold the truth for which we are contending. They maintain an absolute reserve upon the subject. It is not that they would not like to proclaim such a glorious hope. It has exorcised from their own mind many a gloomy spectre of doubt concerning God's love and goodness. Faith in Christianity, to them, would be impossible without it. But they dare not risk the loss of seat-holders and subscribers, whose religious prejudices would be offended, or face the carping and criticism which would ensue.

If ever the voice of conscience reproaches them for their unfaithfulness to truth, they justify their silence by saying that this particular doctrine is not an essential to salvation; or it is accounted, as in the cases of several I know, an *esoteric* truth, which, while ourselves holding, we are not called upon to impart to others. And so hundreds of good and thoughtful men, who with this knowledge would be kept on the side of Christianity, without it, are left to drift into the ranks of Agnosticism and Materialism.

All I ask of any one into whose hands this little

work may fall, is to read on patiently and thought-
fully to the end, and with the Bible correctly translated beside him, to "prove all things," and "hold
fast that which is good" (1 Thess. v. 21)

I shall do with this Deduction as our Church does
with all doctrine, viz., bring it to the test of Holy
Scripture.　I take my stand on the principles of the
Church of England, which places the Word of God
above the opinions of divines, whether those opinions be taken collectively as constituting the decrees
of councils, or, only as the utterances of individual
teachers.

Again, no one abreast with the religious thought
of the day, will deny that this truth concerning the
saving work of Christ beyond the grave, is silently,
but surely, forcing itself upon the minds of men of
all schools of thought in the Church.　To many it
has come as a gleam of cheering sunshine to scare
away the dark shadows lurking in the theology of
the past.　The advance of knowledge and a better
translation of the original text of Scripture, are caus-
ing many erroneous ideas of the past to disappear,
and overlooked truths to be realized.

The faith of thoughtful men has been assailed and threatened by ugly doubts and questionings about God and God's goodness, and the recognition of this truth has answered their doubts and questionings, and kept them to their Christian moorings, and so saved them from drifting out upon the troubled sea of unbelief. To such it has seemed little short of a fresh revelation from God. And yet it is no new truth. It is no modern addition to the glorious Gospel of our Lord Jesus Christ. It is an old truth; just as old as the Gospel itself. It is so much a part of that Gospel, that, were it shown to be otherwise, for many that Gospel would cease to be a Gospel at all. It is no hazy speculation engendered by the gentler spirit and more sympathetic character of this twentieth century. It dates from an epoch which is the starting-point of all that makes us in spirit and character better than our forefathers It is a truth which lies crystallized in the words of our Lord and His Apostles, and it was grasped by the Fathers of the early Eastern Church. But it has been lost sight of, or nearly so, by the Western Church for centuries. This truth has its roots in the eternal principles of love, compassion and mercy, and it can only appeal to the minds of men who are under the sway of those principles.

It has been lost sight of, because men have lacked the moral disposition necessary for its perception. Apostolic men perceived it, because the Apostolic Church was permeated with the spirit of love and mercy.   The Church of later ages failed to perceive it, for the reason that her history has been stained by deeds of cruelty and bloodshed, and disfigured by narrowness and intolerance.   The mental atmosphere of men so unloving as to sanction the Inquisition, and so exclusive as to endorse Calvinism, was such that by no possibility could the perception of this truth be kept alive.   Happily, the truth remained in spite of man's failure to perceive it. Happily, the Church of Christ, to-day, is exhibiting more of the spirit of her Master than she has done for hundreds of years; and, as a consequence, this magnificent truth so long obscured is becoming recognized.

The truth of our fifth Deduction established by two considerations.

I. God's attitude toward the human race, as portrayed by the writers of Scripture, makes it a *necessity* that there should be a preaching of the Gospel in the Intermediate-life.

When God devised the scheme of Redemption, He contemplated humanity *as a whole.*

It was no expedient whereby only a limited number of the human race should be brought within the pale of salvation, and the remainder left outside. That, alas! has been taught by men who have looked at the word "election" through the smoky glass of Calvinism. It by no means follows that because God chooses to "elect" some to Christian privileges in this Earth-life, and to distinguished honor in the Life Beyond, in order that He, through them, may bless others, that those others outside this "Election" are excluded from salvation.   The Jews were God's elect people, and the Gentiles were not; but the door of the Kingdom of Heaven was not barred against the latter on that account. The Church of Christ is described as being God's "elect" people, and she is declared to be the "*First-Fruits* of His creatures" (James i. 18), but

she will not be the *sum-total* of the harvest of redemption.   The word itself implies that the "First-
Fruits" are no more than the pledge of a far
greater ingathering to follow.

The Son of God became incarnate, in order that
the entire human race might be saved.   He placed
the attainment of everlasting life within the reach
of every human creature who had come, or would
come into existence.   No one, whatever his environment, is outside God's love.

Of no person is it true that God does not wish
him to be saved.

The Scripture is very emphatic on this point.
"God so loved *the world* that He gave His only
begotten Son" (John iii. 16); "God sent not His
Son into the world to condemn the world, but that
the world through Him might be saved" (v. 17);
"God was in Christ reconciling *the world* unto
Himself" (2 Cor. v. 19); "God also hath highly
exalted Him, and given Him a name which is above
every name, that at the name of Jesus *every knee*
should bow" (Phil. ii. 10); "That in the dispensation of the fulness of times, He (God) might gather

together in one *all things* in Christ, both which are
in heaven and which are on earth " (Eph. i. 10);
" Having made peace through the blood of His
Cross by Him to reconcile *all things* unto Himself "
(Col. i. 20); " The Father sent the Son to be the
Saviour of *the world* " (1 John iv. 14); " This is
good and acceptable in the sight of God our Saviour, who will have *all men* to be saved and to
come unto the knowledge of the truth " (1 Tim.
ii. 4); " That God may be all *in all* " (1 Cor.
xv. 28).

These passages, out of a great many more, surely
prove that the plan of salvation was devised with
no thought of God's exclusion from it of any member of the human race.

But the above representation of God is untrue in
the face of the millions who leave the Earth-life
without so much as hearing the Gospel, if there be
no preaching of that Gospel in the Intermediate-
life.

It is quite certain that the Almighty has placed it
in the power of but a few, comparatively, to sav-
ingly know Christ, this side of the grave. If He

wills that *all men* should be saved, all, at least, will be offered that salvation, and if the offer has not been made in the Earth-life, it must be in the Unseen-life, unless we are prepared to say that the sacred writers have overstated God's love and wishes toward our race. Hence the truthfulness of the Bible itself is bound up with the truth contained in this fifth Deduction.

II. The other consideration is, that the *office* and *position* assigned to our Lord by the writers of Scripture, makes it a *necessity*, also, that there should be this preaching of the Gospel in the Intermediate-life.

How is our Lord represented in Holy Scripture? As "the Saviour of *all men*, especially of those that believe" (1 Tim. iv. 10); "a ransom *for all*, to be testified in due time" (1 Tim. ii. 6); "the propitiation for our sins; and not for ours only, but also for the sins of the *whole world*" (1 John ii. 2); "the Lamb of God which taketh away the sin of *the world*" (John i. 29).

Further, in speaking of Himself, Christ said, "The bread that I will give is My flesh, which I

will give for the life of *the world*" (John vi. 5);
"I, if I be lifted up from the earth, will draw *all
men* unto Me" (John xii. 32); while His last words
spoken on earth were, "Go ye into *all the world*,
and preach the Gospel to *every creature*" (Mark
xvi. 15).

Clearly, then, Christ cannot be "the Saviour of
all men," unless *all* men be vouchsafed, either here,
or hereafter, a fair chance of embracing the benefits
which He offers. If only one were to perish, because the knowledge of salvation through Jesus had
been withheld, then His claim to be "the propitiation for the sins of the *whole world*" must be re-
linquished.

And yet untold millions die without so much as
even hearing Christ's name. If there be no preaching of Him in the Unseen-life, then they can never
know Him, and there can be no possibility of salvation for them; and the sacred writers were guilty
of exaggeration, when they assigned to Christ the
position of "the Saviour of *all* men."

Hence we see that the truthfulness of the writers
of the New Testament, and of Christ Himself, is

bound up with the truth contained in this fifth Deduction.

In order that we may the better realize the weightiness of these two foregoing conclusions, and, moreover, show that we have not exaggerated in saying that a preaching of the Gospel in Hades is a *necessity*, if God's attitude, and Christ's position toward man be such as the Bible describes, let us honestly consider *the position of the human race in past ages, and now, as to its chances of salvation.*

I will premise the following, which no Christian reader, in whatever other respect he may differ from me, will refuse to grant.

(*a*) That no one can attain salvation apart from a knowledge of God, and of His love and mercy in Christ. Our Lord's words are very decisive on this point. "This is life eternal, that they may *know* Thee the only true God, and Jesus Christ whom Thou hast sent" (John xvii. 3)

(*b*) That this knowledge cannot be obtained unless communicated to us. Christ, in order to communicate it, founded a Church, and commissioned

His followers to "go into all the world and preach" (Mark xvi. 15).

(*c*) That those who have this knowledge can be in a state of salvation, while those who do not possess it cannot be.

(*d*) That God loves the world, and is "not willing that any should perish" (2 Peter iii. 9).

Now, suppose that an inhabitant of one of the planets were to be transported to this earth. He is told, we will imagine, about man's fall, and those truths concerning his recovery which I have just enumerated; but he is also told that there is no possibility of salvation for man, if he be not brought into that condition this side of the grave; that though man will continue his existence in an Intermediate-life, there will be no preaching of the Gospel there.

What, think you, would that visitor count on finding, as he looked around upon men and their prospects of salvation ? He would certainly expect from what had been said about God's love, and Christ's office, that to every human creature on this earth the offer of salvation *had been*, or *was being* made.

if it were hinted to him that the Church had so badly carried out the command of her Divine Master, that, instead of millions, there were only thousands of missionaries, that would only lead him to be on the lookout for angels, instead of men, as preachers in the out-of-the-way places of the earth. It would never strike him that God would let a magnificent work of love and mercy be spoilt because men were not energetic enough. Were he told that even *one* man had lost eternal life because he had been so circumstanced as to die before knowing anything about it, his reply to his informer would be that he must be mistaken; it could not be so; that if there be no preaching in the next life, the man must have been offered salvation in this, since God "will have *all* men to be saved."

If he were told that the great bulk of mankind had lost eternal life because their earthly environment was such as to make it impossible for them to be Christians, then I think he would open his eyes in amazement, and go back to his sphere, and tell his brother Intelligences that he had found the theologians of earth the most extraordinarily illogical beings in existence; that in one breath they affirm that God loves *the world*, and in the next breath deny it, by saying that His love cannot exercise itself outside a miserable little limit which *they*, not *He*, has affixed.

This is not a far-fetched illustration. If men's minds had not become warped by long familiarity with a teaching essentially narrow and pitiless, it would be impossible for any thoughtful person, with an open Bible before him, to conceive the idea that the eternal destiny of *all* is irreversibly fixed at the moment of death. Those who hold such an opinion do not realize what it involves.

Think of the teeming myriads of human beings who, from the remote centuries to the present time, have lived and died. The number is inconceivable.

Scores of millions of people die every year. Add to the death-rate of one year that of thousands of years. The number of leaves on every tree in the world does not represent the sum total.

Think, as regards this vast aggregate, that the bulk has been outside the little area of Christian privileges; that, certainly, not more than one in every ten thousand has heard of God's love and Christ's salvation; and that, having died in this ignorance, these persons are beyond the range of redemption. How awful! How inexpressibly saddening! What an unsatisfactory ending for a scheme of mercy which was devised in contemplation of our race *as a whole*, and announced by the Saviour Himself as such!

Import into the consideration, moreover, the fact that every one of these unfortunate beings stands as much in need of being saved as we do; and they are as capable of being "children of light" as we are. That many of them, indeed, have done deeds of heroism and exhibited traits of character which may well put us Christians to the blush, and make us ask whether they are not more fit for eternal life than we are.

Oh! ye makers and supporters of a theology, which is stamped with the name of Christ, but does not reflect His spirit, how can ye think that a world which God loves, and for which Christ died, must perish (except in so far as concerns a few), because it does not possess that which God, in this life, has never given it a chance of having!

And yet it must be so, if there be no preaching of the Gospel in the Intermediate-life.

Will ye not read into the words of the Church's great theologian, St. Paul, what ye have hitherto failed to note: that Christ, the "Ransom for *all*, *is to be testified in due time*" (1 Tim. ii. 6), and that for the greater proportion of the human race, that "due time" must be the Intermediate-life!

But again, think of the earthly environment of hundreds of thousands who have lived, and are living, in what we call Christian countries. Will any one venture to say, if the possibility of salvation beyond the grave be denied, that God has dealt either lovingly, or even fairly, with *all* whose lot has been cast, for example, in India or China, to say nothing of Christian Europe, or favored England?

In denying our position, is it possible in regard to these millions, to say, "God loves them; Christ died to save them"? I think not.

Take a case in point. It is but a sample of many

of which I have had experience during a four years' ministry in the East of London.

Here is a fellow creature, born in a garret, in a dismal, wretched slum. He is the outcome of drink, that is to say, he would never have been begotten, but that the immoral passions of his parents had been inflamed by drunkenness. He was an interloper, a burden, and a disgrace, and he was made to feel it. Unloved, uncared for, left to shift for himself, he gravitated to the gutter, and never so much as heard the name of God or Christ, except on the lips of profanity.

Years passed over his head. The child of neglect became the boy of fifteen, who picked up a miserable pittance by carrying parcels in the streets. He knew nothing about salvation. Nobody had told him of it. The doors of the Sunday-school were closed against him. He was too ragged and disreputable. Once, years ago, on a bitter cold night, the warm lights of a church had attracted him. He had ventured to peep inside the porch, but a gorgeous beadle had made him beat a quick retreat. He had never been since. He had come to the conclusion that churches were not for " the likes of him."

A few more years glided away. It was winter-time, and a murky London fog enwrapped every-thing in gloom. He was half-frozen, hungry, wretched. He stepped off the curb-stone to cross the road.

There was a shout; a cry of horror from the by-standers. The wheel of a heavily-laden wagon had crushed him into eternity.

Dare we, as we bend over the poor, disfigured wreck of humanity, and think of our cushioned pew and Christian privileges, say that there ought *not* to be a preaching of the Gospel to him in the Unseen-life ? If we can say it, is our Christianity anything more than a lifeless creed, without the spirit of Christ ?

Again, there are numbers living in lands where Christ is preached, whose status is not that of the outcast, to whom God's truth has never really been presented.

Take the case of the uneducated poor in many country districts, a hundred years ago. Unable to

read; untrained for thinking; doomed to listen to
dull, prosy sermons, which converted pews into
sleeping boxes; and accustomed, from infancy, to
see the dust of neglect and dreariness lie thick on
everything connected with religion, what chance
was there for the poor farm-laborer of finding God
in this life? Very little, surely!

Suppose he died as he had lived—insensible to
Divine realities, because they had never been
brought home to his consciousness—what then?
Ask the one who presumes to say to God's Love,
"Thus far shalt thou come; but no further." You
know the terrible answer. Yes; but which is the
more in harmony with Divine Love—that, in the
Intermediate-life, an earnest preacher should show
that man the truth, as it had never before been
shown him, or that God should let him perish for
lack of that truth, the victim of an apathetic
Church?

Again, at a higher social level than that of the
uneducated agriculturalist, there have been other
persons in Christian lands to whom God's truth has
also never really been presented. I am referring to

persons of education and thought, who, good and pure in their life, have felt it to be a paramount duty not to dismiss the question of religion without enquiry and investigation. Pure in heart they have been, so far as moral disposition is concerned, in a favorable condition for perceiving God and His truth.

They have turned for enlightenment to the recognized leaders of religious thought. They have gone, *e. g.*, to the Calvinist, and what has he told them? From a terminology in which the expressions "Divine sovereignty," "Election," and "Reprobation" have figured, he has gathered three things:—that God is a Being who arbitrarily selects a few upon whom to confer the blessing of eternal life; that He heartlessly abandons the rest to drift into everlasting torment; and in regard to the latter, that He brings them into existence to compass that end.

The seeker after God is disappointed. The God he wanted to find is shown to be infinitely worse than himself Christianity is not what he had hoped it might be. He cannot be mistaken; he has the word of Christian teachers themselves.

And so he cannot, unless he strangle his conception of goodness, be a Christian. He will go on trying to be noble and good without subscribing to such a terrible creed. He stands aloof from the Christ of so-called orthodoxy.

At last he dies, and some, if they could, would write over his tomb the word " Lost."

Stay! That man might have been a lover of God, and a sincere believer in the Lord Jesus Christ, whose beautiful character he reflected, perhaps, better than we do, had his teachers been less infected with barbaric thought. Will you say that Christ, so misrepresented and maligned, who said He would leave the ninety and nine sheep and go after the one who has gone astray, will make no effort hereafter to sweep away the misconception from that man's mind?

And yet you must say that if you deny a preaching in the Intermediate-life.

Thus are we driven to the conclusion that the world has been, and is, so circumstanced in regard to God's design of salvation as to make a preaching of the Gospel in the Intermediate-life a *necessity*.

If this be not conceded, then we have no alternative but to view the statements of the Bible respecting God's love, and Christ's office, as the exaggerated utterances of men carried over the confines of truthfulness by their too kindly feelings.

Whether this latter be compatible with a belief in Divine Inspiration, I leave my reader to decide.

The direct statements of Scripture in establishment of our fifth Deduction.

There may be some who say that the passages to which we have appealed in support of our argument, go no further than to show the *likelihood* of there being a preaching of the Gospel in the Unseen-life. They do not positively state that such actually is the case. Is there no *direct* statement in the Bible, sufficiently plain and unequivocal, to set the question completely at rest? Has no inspired writer been permitted to lift the veil which shrouds the Hereafter, so that we may be quite sure that our glorious hope is a certainty?

Yes. St. Peter has done so. I must refer to his words again, although I have had occasion already to quote them in connection with Proposition III.

The passages are:—1 Peter iii. 18–20, quoted as they stand in the Greek. "Christ also hath once suffered for sins, the just for the unjust, that He might bring us to God, having been put to death in the flesh, but quickened in the spirit; in which (*i. e.*, in His Spirit condition) also He went and preached unto the spirits in prison (Greek, "in *keeping* "); who once were disobedient, when once the long-suffering of God waited in the days of Noah." And, in close connection with this passage, 1 Peter iv. 6. "For this cause was the Gospel preached also to them that are dead, that they might be judged according to men in the flesh, but live according to God in the spirit."

The first of these two passages is a statement of fact. As much so as the words which declare that Christ discoursed to a multitude on a mountain-side, or by the Lake of Galilee, or that St. Paul addressed the men of Athens on Mars' Hill. There is need to insist upon this, because an attempt has been made to denude this passage of its significance by making " the spirits in prison " merely to mean persons on this earth who are living in the bonds of sin.

What are the real facts presented here?

That, ages ago, a world of disobedient men and women, insensible to the claims of righteousness, were swept from out the Earth-life by the terrible waters of the Flood; and passed, unsaved, into the Intermediate-life. There, for centuries, they remained "in keeping"; and the words—"who once were disobedient"—imply that the awful judgment which had befallen them, had not been without the effect of producing in them the spirit of obedience.

As with Dives in Hades, the discipline of the Unseen World had developed new and better traits of character.

In due time, "the Saviour of all men," and, consequently, the One capable of being *their* Saviour, was crucified on Calvary, and His spirit, as do the spirits of all, passed at physical death into the Unseen World. In that spirit, severed from His lifeless Body, Jesus preached to these very beings who had preceded Him to that World.

What He preached, and *for what reason* He preached, is told us in the second of the passages.

Christ preached the glad tidings of salvation to them. " For for this cause was the *Gospel* preached also to them that are dead."

The word " dead," as I have shown in another place, could only refer to the Antediluvians' physical condition; since there would be no sense in preaching to beings who had passed out of existence.

Christ's *object* in preaching was, first, that these persons, at the bar of God's judgment, might stand on the same footing as those to whom salvation by Christ is offered during the Earth-life—" that they might be judged according to men in the flesh," *i.e.*, judged by the *same rule* as others more favorably circumstanced, viz., by the Gospel message itself.

The question upon which the Judgment of mankind will turn, is not whether they have been sinners, but whether they have turned to Christ for pardon and sanctification. This implies that all men must, at least, be told of the Christ to whom they must turn. Professor Godet says, "No human spirit reaches the crucial point of its probation, until it has come into contact with the claims of the Lord Jesus Christ for acception or rejection."

These old-world sinners, however great their wickedness, had never rejected Christ in the sense in which we, to whom He has been preached, may reject Him. Hence, for them to be judged hereafter by the same standard as that by which we and all men will be judged, it was necessary that there should be vouchsafed to them the same opportunity of salvation as has been granted to us.

To imagine otherwise would be to impute unfairness to the Judge of all the earth.

The other object for which Christ preached to these disembodied beings in the Intermediate-life, was that they might "live according to God in the spirit."

In the *flesh*, they had not done so. But the waters which had swept them into destruction, as far as their bodies were concerned, had not launched them into a condition of utter hopelessness.

They had brought upon themselves a terrible judgment; they had, by their wickedness, shaped around them a character which had to be unshaped and remoulded in the Unseen World. But they had not, at the moment of death, turned their back upon the *all* that Divine Love and Pity could offer. There was still a Jesus who might touch a nature which had been insensible to the claims of the mere moral law. There was still the principle of Divine Love in the universe, which might soften a heart which had not known God as we know Him.

The Almighty might slay them, as He afterward slew " Sihon, king of the Amorites, and Og, the king of Bashan," in order to vindicate His eternal law of righteousness; but behind the slaying lay the fact, repeated twenty-six times in one psalm (Psalm cxxxvi.), that " His *mercy* endureth all through the æon."

And it was under the promptings of this mercy that the Lord Jesus Christ preached the Gospel to these men and women; that in the spirit-life, they might " live according to God," and gain what God would have all gain—everlasting life and blessedness.

There have been untold millions who have not known Christ in this life, who have never sunk in degradation so low as these Antediluvians had sunk.

These latter had the claims of righteousness forced upon them by the earnest preaching and consistent conduct of Noah. Millions who have departed this life unsaved, have never had a like advantage.

Will there be no preaching to such in the Intermediate-life? If not, why not? Why this extension of mercy to some, and the denial of it to others who deserve it far more than they did? Will all the sophistries which a teaching engendered of human narrowness can advance, make it right or fair that the Almighty should act thus? Surely not. If the Bible be true, Christ is "the same, yesterday, and to-day, and all through the ages." Consequently, He must have the same yearning concern for unsaved souls as He had when His human Body hung stiffening in death. If, *then*, when human wickedness had assumed its most hideous form, He could go after lost sheep of a race that had but freshly heaped upon Him such indignity and wrong, will He not do so to-day? Can we imagine that God in His judgment of mankind, has grown less fair, and Christ less loving, pitiful, and solicitous?

And so, what St. Peter has revealed impels us to the belief that there will be a preaching of Christ in the Intermediate-life.

The bearing of this Deduction upon Christian thought and experience.

I. *It, alone, enables a thoughtful Christian to maintain an attitude of fearlessness in the face of an attack upon Christianity.*

We who hold the truth contained in this Deduction, dread no assault upon our religion from whatever quarter it may come. No foe can involve us in a moral entanglement from which we cannot extricate ourselves. He may bring forth his most powerful weapons from the armory of unbelief, but we can blunt their edge and turn them against himself. Difficulties which he can adduce, and which threaten to undermine Faith, disappear in the light of this truth. We have an effective answer to the strongest objections against Christianity, viz., those which deal with its *moral* aspects, as affecting the character of God.

But it is not so in the case of those who exclude a magnificent hope by the denial of a

preaching of Christ's Gospel in the Intermediate-
life.

These, in a contest with unbelief, are in a pitiable
plight.   There is many a breach through which the
foeman may enter the citadel of their faith; many a
faulty link in the armor which makes it exceedingly unwise to stand face to face with him.   It
were better for them not to risk an encounter.
They are sure to be worsted.   They cannot bolster
up a creed which violates principles to which all
right-thinking men do homage.   Their only chance
of making themselves religiously comfortable is to
close the doors and windows of their mind against
the wind of hostile criticism, and to forget that it
is wildly beating against the theological fabric
within which they have ensconced themselves.

And this, indeed, is what many sincere Christian
people do.   They have a positive dread as to what
may happen to their faith, should they be subjected
to the ordeal of listening to what may be said
against it.   To them, an unbeliever is a being to be
dreaded, because their theology furnishes no answer to his arguments.   It never seems to strike

them that a Creed upon which hopes for eternity are rested, must be a poor sort of thing not to be able to hold its own against those who can give sound reasons for rejecting it. And so, those of whom we are speaking, if they be educated and thoughtful, feel the disadvantage under which they labor, and wisely, from their standpoint, decline to enter into discussion with those who differ from them.

This is no overstatement. It is much to be regretted in the interests of Divine truth. And yet, if it be accounted an essential for Christianity, to believe that everything in regard to man is determined at the moment of death, and that there is no preaching of the Gospel in the Unseen-life, it were better for one holding this view not to discuss it, nor to think about it. If he do, he will have to relinquish his faith in Christianity. It is a choice between strangling the moral instincts, or remodelling the views concerning Christ's Gospel.

Confront a believer in the theology which we are opposing with one who rejects Christianity.

The latter, we will suppose, is shrewd enough to

detect the weak points in his opponent's creed at which he is most likely to score an advantage. What is the line upon which he will advance to the attack?

He will, first, ask the Christian whether he admits that God is infinitely good, merciful, and just; and really concerned in the welfare and salvation of His creature, man. The answer, of course, will be "Yes." His next question will be, "How is it, then, that nine-tenths of our race are permitted to perish because God has suffered them to be born, and to live, under circumstances where there has not been a ghost of a chance of their being saved? Can this disastrous handicapping of the bulk of humanity, by a God who could, if He liked, order it otherwise, be compatible with conduct which is either good, considerate, or fair?"

What satisfactory answer can the Christian who denies a preaching of the Gospel in the Unseen-life, give to this? None whatever. He may throw dust into the eyes of his own moral perception by propounding a theory of "Divine sovereignty" which, according to him, entitles God to do as He will with His unfortunate creatures; but he knows full well that on the grounds of righteousness and fairness, his adversary has obtained the better of the argument. He leaves the discussion with the uncomfortable sensation that all he was able to say in defence of his theory has but confirmed the unbeliever in his doubt.

Not so is it with us. Confront us with the same opponent. Let him advance the same argument, and we have an answer at hand which can silence all his imputations upon the Almighty's goodness, mercy, and fair-dealing.

Thus, do we become fearless in the presence of unbelief. And only thus.

II. *Our Deduction, alone, enables us to reconcile many of the acts of God's Providence with the thought of His goodness.*

No Christian will deny that many things befall mankind which, being altogether beyond our control, must be viewed either as having been appointed by God, or, at least, permitted by Him. These occurrences we term "Divine Providence."

Nor is the term misapplied, although they be

seen to be the result of natural laws, since God made the laws; provides that they shall work out their ends; and, moreover, could, did He so wish, suspend them in their operations.

Clearly, then, every event beyond the control of man must be assigned to Him. We recognize this when we speak of "visitations of God." We open our newspapers and read of appalling disasters. A sudden squall strikes a vessel under full sail, and capsizing it, buries, within a few moments, three or four hundred sailor-lads in a watery grave. A thunder-storm bursts over farm-laborers working in the fields, or upon little children gathering wild flowers, and in an instant the lightning has scorched one or more of them into eternity. A huge tidal-wave, a cyclone, an earthquake, a subsidence of land, without warning, hurries thousands into destruction.

To the one whose belief requires that the horizon of hope should be bounded by the grave, these things are unutterably perplexing. He shudders at the bare idea of thinking that God is not loving and kind to all His creatures. But how can he reconcile such acts of Providence with the attributes which he ascribes to Him ?

He turns to his Bible, but only reading into its utterances his own preconceptions, he finds nothing there which will scare away the haunting spectre of doubt.

Nay, if following the example of the enemies of Christianity, he reads of certain events recorded in the Old Testament, without letting the light which streams from the inspired words of St. Peter fall upon them, his doubts are likely to become intensified. When, for example, the flood swept sinful men and women into destruction, numbers of little children and infants perished with them. When the earth "opened her mouth and swallowed up" Korah, Dathan and Abiram, all that appertained unto them, "their wives and their sons and their little children," "went down quick into the pit" with them.

How will one who denies the truth for which we are contending, reconcile these facts with the goodness, mercy, or justice of God ? Will not the awful conviction be forced upon him, that however conspicuous these Divine attributes may be in other dealings of God, here, at least, they cannot be traced? How unloving, how unfair, to deprive the unoffending of the chances of salvation because others have sinned! Upon such narratives as these, and upon many events which happen around us, it is impossible to allow the mind to dwell, without either admitting the truth of our Deduction, or of being conscious that we are holding a creed against which our reason and instincts rebel.

Many good persons do hold such a creed, and remain Christians; but it is only accomplished by a persistent drugging of the intellect into a condition of moral insensibility.

I do not mean, as regards their own personal life and conduct, that they are insensible to moral instincts; but it is so, as far as their perception of morality in God is concerned. They themselves may be compassionate and just, and yet ascribe to Infinite Love a line of conduct which would be a disgrace to an Oriental despot.

Such persons present a curious phenomenon. In character, they are superior to their creed; and in practice, better than the God they imagine.

What a striking contrast there is between the mental attitude of those to whom we have referred, and that of ourselves who believe in a preaching of the Gospel in the Intermediate-life. The Providences of God may sadden us, and sober us into becoming more earnest men; they cannot unsteady our faith in His mercy and justice. We have a something which can touch the direst catastrophe, and transmute it into a deed of goodness and blessing.

Take, for instance, the case of the foundering of the training-ship "Eurydice." How terrible the loss of those poor sailor lads!

Yes; but what if, when the Almighty suffered them to be drowned, He only transferred them from one sphere of existence to another; and that His mercy followed them thither!

Had they been permitted to reach manhood, it is possible that the sinful allurements of earth might have so hardened their moral character as to make it very, very difficult for them to attain eternal life; and knowing this, God mercifully removed them to the Unseen-life, in order that the work of salvation in them might be more easily accomplished.

The influence of bad companions, and the disadvantage of an evil environment, might have rendered them insensible to the pleadings of an earthly preacher. And so God placed them in a World where the atmosphere of eternal realities would make them more likely to listen to the message of salvation when preached to them there.

And thus, however terrible, from a human standpoint, the judgment which involves the innocent with the guilty; however heartrending the disaster which closes the earthly career of some who, had they been permitted to live, might have become far better Christians than we are, our faith in God's goodness and justice remains unshaken.

Our belief affords us what the creed of those who differ from us does not afford them. Chained to the horrible thought that the destiny of *every one* is fixed at the moment of death, they are compelled to make God's Providences the point at which His love vanishes. The waves have quenched it; the lightning has blasted it; the earthquake has swallowed it.

But not so do we think. We believe that " the

Lord is good to *all*, and His tender mercies are over *all* His works" (Ps. cxlv. 9); that His yearning desire for man's salvation oversteps the petty, span-long limitation affixed by a loveless theology. The lost sheep may be overtaken by the snow-storm of death before the pitiful Saviour reaches it. But He will not, depend upon it, let the storm turn Him from His purpose. "He will go after that which is lost, until He find it" (Luke xv. 4). The love of God will surely follow the poor drowned sailor, the suffocated miner, and millions who by disaster have been prematurely swept from out the Earth-life into the Intermediate-life.

Does not Christ, who preached the Gospel to sinful Antediluvians that they might "live according to God in the spirit," either Himself, or in the persons of His servants, preach to *them* there? We believe that He does do so, and thus, in face of everything which befalls mankind, we can hold firm to our belief in the love, mercy and justice of God.

III. *Our Deduction invests the duty of Intercessory Prayer with increased significance.*

There is no need to insist upon the necessity for Prayer. It is a duty which has been recognized under every form of religious belief. The Christian instinctively feels that without it his hold on eternal realities is likely to be relaxed, and his moral and spiritual development unlikely to be accomplished. He no more expects that the Christ-life within him will be kept alive without communion with God, than that fish-life can remain without the water, or animal and plant-life without the air. Prayer is the atmosphere in which he "lives, and moves, and has his being." He knows that the more he imbibes it into his spiritual constitution, the more vigorous will he become; the less he does so, the feebler, in his faith and practice, will he be; while, if he does not pray at all, he will probably lose his power of perceiving Divine truth.

But while the necessity for prayer is universally acknowledged, the superiority of Intercessory Prayer is too often insufficiently realized. And yet the latter is as much above all other kind of prayer, as the act of giving is above that of receiving.

And for this reason.

It is quite possible to make prayer degenerate into a mere exercise of selfishness. Many earnest-minded persons pray a great deal; but only for themselves. It is conceivable that a little less of this kind of prayer might even be better for the development of their character.

In the act of Intercessory Prayer, we rise into an atmosphere where selfishness is placed out of its element.

When we pray for others, we put ourselves *en rapport* with God. He is always thinking about others; constantly concerning Himself about their welfare. In Intercession we do the same thing. Consequently, there is an affinity between God's mind and ours. A thousand prayers offered to God, where the consideration of self lies behind them, will never bring us into such near communion with Him as one earnest petition presented on behalf of another.

In this way, Intercessory Prayer is a nobler exercise of the soul than any other prayer can possibly be.

There was a grander majesty, even, about the

Lord Jesus Christ, when He pleaded, "Father, for-
give them," than when He prayed, "Let this cup
pass from Me."

Now, it seems to me that those who deny the
truth of this Deduction, destroy a great deal of the
significance of Intercessory Prayer. They adopt a
theological position which assigns no room for an
answer to most of their prayers for others. They
mark out a little period, viz., the Earth-life of a
man,—beyond which they account an answer impossible; and, as they perfectly well know it to be
more the exception than the rule for the answer to
be vouchsafed *within* that period, they have no alternative but to view the most of their intercessions
as ineffectual. At best, there is only a chance of
God granting what is asked. In nine cases out of
ten, from their standpoint, the utmost that Intercession is likely to bring about, is to raise the peti-
tioner's own moral and spiritual tone.

In other words, more often than not, it fails in its
direct purpose.

Take an instance in point. In our Litany we
pray that God may "have mercy upon *all* men";

and in one of the Occasional Prayers, that He will " be pleased to make His ways known unto *all* sorts and conditions of men." Suppose we pare down the beautiful words, and limit the " all " to mean only those living upon the earth at the time we present the petition. What then ? Within an hour, before ever we leave the church, thousands of souls will have left the Earth-life, with no knowledge, or but an inadequate knowledge, of God vouchsafed to them. There can be no question about that fact. If the mercy and enlightenment for which we pleaded on their behalf will not, under any circumstances, be granted *after death*, why make our intercession so embracive ?

Were we consistent in asking for that which we knew beforehand would not be granted ? Were not the Puritans more logical than Churchmen who deny our Deduction, when the former objected to the clause in the Litany just quoted, on the grounds that, as millions departed this life in an unsaved condition, it was certain God did not mean them to obtain salvation, and that, therefore, it was absurd to ask it for them ?

Take one other instance of how Intercessory Prayer may be robbed of its significance, when there is the denial of the preaching of the Gospel in the Intermediate-life.

A Christian mother, thoroughly earnest, but imperfectly instructed concerning the all of Divine truth, has a son

He, we will suppose, has reached the age of manhood; is affectionate; moral in his life; but not a Christian.

From infancy, she and others have taught him that Christianity is bound up with the doctrine that the destiny of all is irrevocably fixed at death, and that the Almighty will consign the lost to an eternity of unutterable agony. As a boy, he believed it, because his mother said it was so; as a man, he finds himself unable to surrender his conscience to a creed which outrages instincts which he knows to be good. And so, without being actively hostile, he remains indifferent to a religion of which he ignorantly imagines these perversions to be an indispensable part.

The poor mother, believing that he, should he die

with his doubts unremoved, must be inevitably lost,
is profoundly distressed, and, for twenty or thirty
years, makes him the subject of her intercessory
prayers.

At last, perhaps without a moment's warning,
giving no indication that he has become a Christian
in her sense of the word, he is struck down by
Death.   She is heart-broken.   It is too late now!
The last hope is gone!   Her son is eternally lost!

Yes; but what of her intercessions for him!   Are
thirty years of pleading to effect no good?

Was she, then, altogether mistaken in believing
that her Saviour would be faithful to His promise—
"All things, whatsoever ye shall ask in prayer, believing, ye shall receive" (Matt. xxi. 22)?

And yet it must be so, if no enlightenment and
salvation can come to that son in the Unseen-life.

In this way has a crude theology stripped Intercessory Prayer of much of its significance, by leaving us but a *bare* probability that God will answer it.

How very different is it with us who believe that
Jesus is as much a Saviour to men in the Unseen-
life, as to those in the Earth-life.   To us, there is

no inconsistency in praying that God may "have mercy upon *all* men," although we are absolutely sure that the bulk of those for whom we pray will depart this life without the knowledge of Him. If, on the next morning after presenting such a petition, we were to read in our newspaper that, at the moment of praying, a whole continent of beings had suddenly died unsaved, our faith in the efficacy of that petition would not be shaken in the slightest degree. We should admit, of course, with respect to these beings, that God had not answered our prayer *within a certain time :* but we should emphatically decline to say that, because of that, He would not, and could not answer it at all. With the fact before us, in Holy Writ, that Jesus preached to a world unsaved, *after death*, we should view that continent of souls in the Intermediate-life as still within the reach of His mercy. Why should we think Him less pitiful, to-day, than He was eighteen hundred years ago? Instead of feeling that the words of our Church's Litany are hyperbolical, and incapable of fulfilment, we should reiterate them with intenser earnestness.

Then again, were we placed in a like position to that of the mother whom we have instanced, we should not imagine that because our son died without the faith we possess, it was absolutely certain he would be eternally lost. Nor should we think our intercessions had been unavailing.

How do we know that if that man had had more enlightened instructors, and had been offered a theology more worthy of the name of "Gospel," he might not have been a Christian! The chances are he might. How can we suppose that the Jesus who "came not to destroy men's lives, but to save them" (Luke ix. 56), will make no effort, hereafter, to sweep away his misconception of truth!

Moreover, the man was not dead to all sense of goodness.

He did homage in his heart to the character of Jesus, as it was imperfectly reflected by his mother. Many a deed of kindness and self-sacrifice done by him may be remembered and appreciated. Will Christ "break the bruised reed, and quench the smoking flax," till "He send forth judgment unto victory" (Matt. xii. 20)? He says He will not;

that even His judgment against that man is not a
judgment ending in condemnation, but a judgment
" unto *victory*." The Christ will not be defeated in
His purpose of mercy. The reed may be bruised,
and the flax be only smoking; but the Saviour has
infinite resources. His very judgments are Divine
means to mend the one, and to enkindle into flame
the other.

And thus, so far from the man's removal from the
Earth-life making us think that our supplications
for him have been of no avail, we plead all the more
earnestly; confident that one day, in His own good
time, God will answer our prayers, because He
" will have all men to be saved " (1 Tim. ii. 4), and
we shall have been asking " according to His will "
(1 John v. 14).

Truly this enlargement of our thoughts concerning Intercessory Prayer invests it with magnificent
significance.

Viewed as we view it, what, we ask, can so comfort us as we stand beside the dead casket of one
whom we have loved!

What a chilling vacuum there is in our religion,

if, when once the breath has left the body of that one, our supplications must cease!

How contrary to the dictates of charity, if, according to some, we may pray only for "the *faithful* departed"!

How grand and Christlike, if, by our intercessions on earth, we are helping poor lost souls in the Intermediate-life to find their way to the bosom of the Good Shepherd!

IV. *Our Deduction imparts new incentive to work for Christ.*

This new incentive arises from the conviction that earnest efforts made for the salvation of others will yield results *outside the limit usually assigned.*

That limit, many say, is the moment of death; at which if results have not accrued, they will never do so.

We contend that, according to God's Word, the limit within which results are possible must not be affixed at any point short of that magnificent consummation which St. Peter described as the "Restitution of *all* things" (Acts iii. 21), when, ac-

cording to St. Paul, God shall be "all in *all*" (1
Cor. xv. 28).

The difference is enormous. In the one case,
more than half the work done for Christ is practically rendered hopeless. In the other case, none of
it is so. On the one hand, there is only a chance
that a single seed, out of every hundred or thousand
good seeds sown, will germinate. On the other,
that *every* seed may.

Of course the different aspects of things presented by the two views will considerably affect
the worker in the way in which he prosecutes his
work. The one will cause him, at times, to be dis-
heartened and despondent, and he will need the in-
toxicating stimulus of religious excitement to keep
him at his post.

The other will make him calmly persistent, and
uniformly hopeful. Noisy urgings to duty will
rather hinder than help him. He will be undismayed
if results do not appear, because he sees a way in
which God will be able (even when others say it is
impossible), to fulfil His promise—"My word . . .
shall not return unto Me void" (Isa. lv. 11).

The force of these remarks will come home, especially, to those of my brethren, who, like myself, have worked as clergymen in East London, or in similar spheres of duty.

Think of an earnest clergyman whose creed forbids him to hope that any *after death* can be turned to Christ. Full of noble enthusiasm, and eager for the eternal salvation of his parishioners, he commences his work. He preaches, teaches, warns, exhorts, visits from house to house, willing "to spend and be spent," if only he can make men Christians. So he goes on, and at the end of twelve months the good he has done is scarcely appreciable. Ignorance, grinding poverty, and an evil environment, have, as far as he can see, neutralized his efforts. Another year of the same experience. In spite of a sincere wish to the contrary, the conviction begins to force itself upon his mind that much of his work is of no avail. It produces its effect upon him. There is to him less of promise about Christian work than there was. He goes on with his task because he is a good man, and it is a duty; but the impetus arising from great expectations is waning.

Twenty years pass away. Thousands to whom he has ministered have died during that period. In the case of how many of them can he say that he has seen the outcome of his labors? Of but, comparatively, a few. What is his candid estimate of his ministry in the face of his belief that, as concerns the many who have died, no results *will ever come?*

It can be none other than that by far the larger proportion of his work for Christ has yielded nothing.

Can we wonder if Christian energy in such an one should all but die out? His creed in a great measure is responsible for it.

Contrast with this, the advantage possessed by one who can believe that the sphere of Redemption is not bounded by the grave, and that even out of judgment on sin will come forth victory for the saving Christ.

How immeasurably expanded does the horizon of expectation become. Such an one in his work for Christ does not look for anything like a harvest of results until the After-life. Now and again, indeed, he may be rejoiced at the sight of some seed sown by him springing into blade, or even into the unripened ear, before the rest has shown itself above ground.   But that is but an earnest of what he expects will follow.   He knows, as concerning the bulk of "the bread which he is casting upon the waters," that it will be carried on the tide of Time into the ocean of Eternity, and he will not find it until "*after many days*" (Eccles. xi. 1).

When, for example, he sees his instruction given to the children, and his ministration to the adults, yielding no manifest results, for the reason that an evil home-influence, and the foul atmosphere of poverty and squalor, have dulled and blurred all just perception of goodness and truth, he does not account his efforts as so much energy thrown away. Why should he ?

He believes in a God who is not an unsympathizing Exactor, but a Being of infinite love and fairness, who will leave no stone unturned to save a soul from death.

The magnificent picture of Jesus preaching to lost sinners in Hades is ever before his mind's eye.

The word faithfully spoken for the Master "shall not return void." It may have been imperfectly realized, misunderstood, unheeded, forgotten, this side of the grave, but it shall be remembered beyond, and will, in spite of all that some daringly say to the contrary, bring poor, erring, blinded ones to the feet of their Saviour.

With the Gospel invested with this diviner grandeur, the whole complexion of his work for Christ becomes transfigured. Others will be made desponding and half-hearted by a lack of results; he, the more incited to increased activity. Others, like foolish children who are ignorant of the laws of growth and development, will sow seeds, and grow disappointed with their gardening, because the green blades do not immediately show themselves; he will go on with the sowing, content to wait. Full well does he know that many a seed which has not germinated in the Earth-life, on account of the freezing air of an unfavorable environment, will bring forth fruit an hundredfold in the sunnier circumstances of the Unseen-life.

Many of the clergy and laity whom I know, conspicuous for their untiring energy and self-denial in their labors for Christ among the wretched and outcast, hold the truth embodied in this fifth Deduction. And some of them have acknowledged to me that but for the thought of a preaching of the Gospel hereafter, under circumstances where there is a possibility of salvation, such as can hardly be said for many to exist here, the incentive for work would be lost.

V. *Our Deduction makes it probable that the mission of the Church of Christ is a far greater one than is generally supposed.*

The Church is an Institution founded by our Lord Jesus Christ to be the living witness of the truth which He came to reveal, and the medium by which that truth shall be made known to mankind.

She is no mere eclectic association formed for the benefit of those who constitute her. She is not a privileged community of Divine favorites, with no relation to the great outside world, except in so far as that world supplies the material by which she can be kept in existence. Many have viewed her in this light, but they have been mistaken. She exists for a purpose. That purpose is, that having first received Christ's blessings of salvation, she shall be the channel through which they shall be offered to all outside her pale. She was founded to bless the whole human race.

That is perfectly plain from the last earthly words spoken by her Founder. "Go ye into all the world and preach the Gospel to *every creature*" (Mark xvi. 15). Her commission is to give effect to what God in His love has done for the world, by bringing the knowledge of salvation to every member of the human family. As far as we know from the statements of the Bible, no knowledge of salvation will ever come to man apart from the instrumentality of man. He, not angels, has been told oft to carry the water of life to perishing mortals. Consequently, every privilege which the Church enjoys has been granted in order that she may the better discharge the office for which she was created.

Now, if we adopt the idea that the work of salvation is restricted, to this side of the grave; if, in other words, the hope of redemption for the un-

saved dies when physical dissolution overtakes
them, we are driven, perforce, to admit that the
Church's mission does not extend beyond this
world. Although she herself, in the persons of
those who constitute her, is partly in the Earth-life,
and partly in the Intermediate-life, yet she can do
absolutely nothing for the vast majority who have
crossed the border-line which divides the Seen from
the Unseen.

The following illustration will serve to show the
unreasonableness of the idea. Suppose that a king
of unbounded sympathy and unlimited resources,
formed in one part of his dominions a great society
for the alleviation of distress which existed among
his subjects. Imagine him, without either breaking
up the Society, or indicating that the work is not to
be continued, removing the greater number of its
members into another district of his empire, where
distress is even more widespread than in the locality where they had hitherto been stationed. What
should we say if it were told us that the great
Society does nothing in the way of relief, except in
the smaller of the two areas of suffering ? Should

we not declare that the king was not carrying out the purpose for which the Society was formed? Why weaken the good work, by taking away so many of the members from a place where they are so badly wanted, and placing them in a spot where, although there is plenty of scope, they must not labor for the cause!

And yet that is the light in which the mission of the Church of Christ is regarded by very many. Millions who constitute her have gone into the Unseen World. They still belong to her; her commission of mercy has never been revoked; and yet with myriads of unsaved souls pouring into that World, it is supposed that they have nothing to do. Because God has given them rest from painful earthly labors, they, forsooth, are thought to be whiling away centuries in a state of unconcern for any but themselves.

Let us see what this restricted view of the Church's function involves. How can it be reconciled with our Lord's words, " Preach the Gospel to *every creature*" ? If the preaching only embraces a work to be done by the Church *while located on earth*, then surely we are driven to admit that our Saviour, in giving the command, either was unable to foresee what the actual condition of mankind in regard to the prospects of salvation would be, or if He knew this, He gave an impracticable commission to His Church. If we deny that she has a ministry in the Intermediate-life, we are shut up to one of these two conclusions.

Suppose the expression "every creature" be made to exclude all who had previously passed out of the Earth-life, and to include only those who at the time the words were spoken were living, or would live, in this world. Did Christ not know that millions would die without so much as even hearing His name? Was He not aware that, for more than fourteen hundred years, His Church would be ignorant of the very existence of the human life teeming upon the vast continent of America? Did He not foresee that, in the twentieth century, the Church in making a map of her missionary work, would have to mark black the greater part of it as the territory of paganism?

And yet He said "Preach to *every creature*." Are

we prepared to say that the words were the outcome of a too enthusiastic optimism; that Christ,
unable to read the future, thought man's prospects
of salvation would be better than they have actually
been?

We shudder at such a suggestion; and yet the
passage read in the light of subsequent history
warrants it, if there be no preaching in the Intermediate-life. The Gospel has not been preached in
this world to *one* out of every ten thousand
creatures.

Again, our Lord's command was an altogether
impracticable one, unless He intended His Church to
continue the preaching of the Gospel in the Unseen-
life. How, otherwise, was it possible to obey it?
For centuries the number of those who composed
the Church were but a handful as contrasted with
the world's population. If every Christian had been
a St. Paul, millions would have been inaccessible to
the preachers, on account of the difficulties of loco-
motion, and the fact that one-half of the globe was
then unknown. Even supposing that, after fifty
years from Christ's ascension, the Church had been

competent to fulfil the mission intrusted to her, during that fifty years, untold millions would have died without hearing the Gospel.

And yet the command was "Preach to *every creature*." Was our Lord assigning an impossible task? Instead of "*every* creature," did He only mean a very small number? We cannot believe this without remodeling our ideas of Him.

But the admission of the truth of our fifth Deduction extricates us from the theological difficulties indicated above. The future earthly condition of the human race was not hidden from Christ, nor did He give an impracticable commission. What He commanded He meant. His Church would preach to "*every* creature."

Divine Providence might so order the lot of man that the majority would never hear His message of mercy in this life; but that was to be no bar to their doing so in another. Bodily dissolution would be but a change of locality and surroundings, both to preachers and hearers. The reach of the preaching was conterminable with the stretch of the love which embraced "*the world*." His Church would preach the Gospel in the Intermediate-life, and its mission, incapable of fulfilment here, would be accomplished there.

It is in this way that we are alone able to rightly estimate the grandeur of the Church's mission.

Instead of being an Institution wholly inadequate for the work she was meant to do, she is invested with a Divine potentiality for blessing the whole race of man. Beneath the light of our Deduction we can understand St. Paul's utterances concerning her; that to her God has "made known the mystery of His will, according to His good pleasure which He hath purposed in Himself; that in the dispensation of the fulness of times He might gather together in one *all things* in Christ, both which are in heaven and which are on earth . . . that we should be to the praise of His glory who first trusted in Christ; . . . to the intent that now unto the principalities and powers in heavenly places might be known *by the Church* the manifold wisdom of God according to the purpose of the ages which He purposed in Christ Jesus our Lord" (Eph. i. 9, 10, 12; and iii. 10 and 11).

What a different complexion is put upon religion itself by this truth. Without it, our Creed is far short of what we could wish. There is a disquieting sense that much is unsatisfactory.

It is so appallingly dreadful to imagine that the greater portion of our fellow-creatures have gone unsaved into the Unseen-life, and will be lost, because no one has told them of their Saviour, or because preachers and teachers have misrepresented His Gospel.

We tremble to think about it, and yet, at the same time we are so constituted that it is difficult to acquire that tone of unthinking religionism which alone can save us from drifting into either infidelity, melancholy, or insanity.

But everything is changed by the thought that Christ's Church is preaching her Master's Gospel in the Intermediate-life. The sense of unsatisfactoriness vanishes as a vision of vast possibilities looms into view. Be the earthly environment of men as black and unpromising as it may, behind it is the sunshine of God's love and fairness, and the fact that at the Great Consummation—the " Restitution of all things "—there will be no creature to whom salvation has not been preached.

And so as I look at the Church of Christ on earth, I am disappointed. Some of us are half-hearted in our work; others, not working at all. Some, longing to serve the Master, cannot do so as they would, because the cross of ill-health, or trouble has been laid upon them. Others, alas! by their imperfect presentment of truth, and by their manner do not attract to the Saviour.

And then I think of the Church of Christ in the Intermediate-life, and am satisfied; for a magnificent contrast presents itself. All of that Church there are preaching, teaching, straining every energy to woo to Christ the ones who had been unfavored on earth. The half-heartedness, the hindrances and the ignorance, have disappeared in the reality, the opportunities and the clearer light of a Higher Sphere.

But there are some who will ask—If it be believed that the Church continues her preaching of the Gospel in the Intermediate-life, will it not make her members, in the Earth-life, careless and less ener-

getic in the carrying out of her Lord's command?

Our answer to this is, "Assuredly not; it will
have a contrary effect."   Nothing is more certain to
make men half-hearted and neglectful in any task
assigned to them, than to think that it can never be
accomplished.   What boy at school would be as-
siduous in his studies, had he the fixed conviction
that he could never become wise!   What soldier
would be enthusiastic to fight, or captain to lead,
knowing beforehand that victory was impossible!

The surest way of making men zealous and inde-
fatigable in a work is to convince them that it can
be done.   The spur is then given to activity.
America was discovered, because Columbus was,
first, sure that there must be land in the far west;
and, next, that it would be possible for him to find
it.   The Alps have been bored, the earth encircled
with cable, and thousands of other marvellous results of energy achieved, solely for the reason that
the energy was enkindled by the conviction that
the results were possible.

In regard to the Church of Christ, limit her preaching of the Gospel to this world, and what have you done? You have made the command given to her an impracticable one. It is impossible, in this Life, to preach to "*every creature.*"

However zealous she may be, there will be the paralyzing influence on her work arising from the knowledge that millions are losing eternal life, because God has placed upon her a responsibility greater than she can possibly sustain. Is not such a reflection sufficient to damp her ardor, and lower her estimate of her mission to mankind? Has it not, in fact, done so? Is not the present age, which is less disfigured than preceding ages by narrowness of doctrine, more conspicuous for missionary enterprise?

Thus, we have no hesitation in saying, that to believe that the Church of Christ will continue to preach her Master's Gospel in the Intermediate-life, so far from making us careless and less energetic in Evangelistic work, will afford a magnificent incentive to further effort. The thought that the fulfilment of the Church's mission has been guaranteed by the fiat of Omnipotence, will extinguish the dis-heartenment which is engendered from the doubt of success.

We shall be doubly anxious to bear an honorable part in a glorious Consummation.

Conscious that upon Her has been laid the dis-tinguished honor of being linked with God in a purpose of Love toward a lost race, and humbled by the thought of how little she has yet done toward the fulfilment of that purpose, the Church will seek, by greater zeal, to justify her existence.

For she will know that when the Intermediate-life shall have ended, and the Great " Restitution " shall have come, of Her it will be said, " She has preached the Gospel to *every creature.*"

APPENDIX.

The bearing of Deduction V. upon the subject
of Future Punishments, and God's "Purpose of
the ages."

THE belief that Christ's Gospel is preached in the
Intermediate-Life does not involve a denial of punishment for sin and impenitence after death. It is
needful to affirm this, because many earnest seekers
after truth hesitate to accept the glorious hope contained in the thought of *post-mortem* evangelization,
owing to the false idea that it excludes, or pares
away, a truth that is very clearly revealed in the
Bible, viz., that the consequences of evil will be
reaped in a world beyond.

Those persons, especially, who believe in, or
think they believe in, the terrible doctrine of unending suffering, not infrequently accuse us who hold
what is known as "the larger hope," first, of min-

imizing evil, and next, of encouraging men to esteem lightly the threatened judgments of God.   We
do nothing of the kind.

For one or two very strong and unanswerable
reasons we reject the doctrine of an everlasting
hell.   We view it as the offspring of an unhealthy
and distorted imagination, and as a supposition that
outrages all moral instincts and ideas of goodness.
In character the doctrine is such that it is impossible
for it to enlist either intellectual or moral assent;
and although it has commanded the *credulity* of
thousands, not one has ever risen to the attitude of
faith in regard to it.

Those who accept it, can only do so by chloro-
forming their mind into insensibility as to what it
implies.   A thorough belief in it could only land a
person (as it has done hundreds) in a mad house.

Again, we account the doctrine to be an awful
slander on the character of God.   It represents Him
whose name is "Love" as being more implacable
and insensible to His creatures' tortures than the
most horrible monster ever invented by pagan
imagination.   Lastly, we reject the doctrine, be-

cause it rests on no better foundation than a few mistranslated words in the Bible; and flatly contradicts hundreds of passages to which attention will be called in later pages.

But while taking this position in regard to a doctrine which has been in the past considered, and is even now considered by many, to be an essential element of the Christian faith, we by no means deny that there is, in the world beyond, a very real and awful judgment upon all sin and impenitence. To us the words of Christ are too emphatic to be mistaken. He spoke of "the darkness without"; of a "weeping and gnashing of teeth"; of a "Gehenna of fire"; of an "aionial pruning" (*i. e.*, the painful discipline of an age); and of a "prison" from which should be no release until "the uttermost farthing" shall have been paid. We think that in the words—"Whatsoever a man soweth, *that* shall he also reap"—is proclaimed an inviolable law of God, framed and enforced for the benefit of His universe; which no person, Christian, or non-Christian, can possibly evade; and that experience and discipline, bitter and searching, must be the

inevitable outcome of an earth-life of wrong-doing.

We do not *minimize* evil.

Those who hold the doctrine of an everlasting
hell seem to us to commit that error.

We regard evil as being such a hateful thing in
the sight of a Father-God who loves all His creatures, that we cannot believe He will tolerate a
gigantic hell of it forever and ever.

Nor does our teaching encourage men to esteem
lightly the threatened judgments of God.

The doctrine we oppose has had that effect, by
creating in the minds of irreligious men the idea
that the punishment of sin, as preached by some
theologians, is so inconceivably horrible and unjust,
that it cannot possibly be true. Thousands, in consequence, have gone to the extreme of not believing
in any future retribution at all. Tell a disobedient
boy that you will cut his head off, or burn him
alive, if he persists in his wrong-doing, and the
probability is he will disregard your threats, on the
ground that he knows the punishment to be too
atrocious ever to be inflicted. Threaten him, on

the other hand, with a punishment that he knows
to be reasonable and just, and he is likely to be
affected thereby. Never was the doctrine of everlasting hell more vigorously set forth in all its
naked repulsiveness than at the time when the
Puritan influence was in the ascendancy in this
country; and yet the succeeding age was characterized by the grossest irreligion, profligacy and vice
One has only to note how lightly and thoughtlessly
the words "Hell" and "Damn" are used by the
masses, to see how little the so-called "orthodox"
teaching, symbolized by those words, has im-
pressed and affected mankind.

To the men and women who show by lives of
sin and indifference that they disregard the future
judgments of God, we say—"There may be an excuse for you in esteeming lightly the threatenings
of God, when those threatenings are made to be of
such a character as to outrage your reason, shock
your sense of justice, and render it impossible for
you to believe them; but you have no such excuse,
when we show you that all God's punishments,
however severe, are yet reasonable, and compatible

with His character as a God of *righteousness* and a
Father of *Love.*"—Thus, we do not deny a future
punishment for sin ; but we differ very fundamen-
tally from those who regard it in the lurid light of
the doctrine of unending woe. On this point,
they and we are at the opposite poles of thought.
They view it as vindictive, hopeless and everlasting;
we, on the contrary, are convinced that it is
Fatherly, *remedial*, and *terminable*. The difference
is enormous. Are they, or are we, right ? If the
assumption be correct that the door of Divine love
and mercy is forever closed and barred against the
sinner when he departs this life, and that the judgment overtaking him in the world beyond will be
irremedial and final, then, of course, the deduction
as to *post-mortem* evangelization and recovery cannot stand. In that case, a preaching of Christ's
Gospel would be useless, or worse. On the other
hand, if all God's future punishments be fatherly
and remedial—as we, in the light of the Scriptures
correctly translated, believe them to be—then, assuredly, the thought of a preaching of the Gospel
after death will commend itself to our reason as

being both fitting and probable. Yes, and the thought will be as a glorious ray of Divine sunlight, dispersing that black cloud of blank hopelessness that has for centuries made gloomy and depressing the religion of Jesus. There are hundreds of thousands of Christians who cannot form any idea of future punishment, apart from its being everlasting and hopeless.

The terms "*eternal* judgment" and "*eternal* punishment," have been dinned into their ears from infancy, and they are unaware of the fact that "eternal," is not a correct translation of the original Greek word *αἰώνιος;* and moreover, that this word, "eternal" denotes without beginning as well as without end, and is misapplied to anything that is not beginningless. Again, there are hosts of earnest seekers after God and truth (as numbers of letters sent to me testify), whose acceptance of the Gospel of Christ is barred by this doctrine of everlasting punishment. They suppose it to be a part of the teaching of the Saviour ; and they cannot embrace a religion which requires assent to something that shocks all their moral instincts. For the sake of such persons, it seems only right that we should examine this doctrine; that we should show them what it really is, and upon what foundation it has been built. Thus, and only thus, will they be brought to see that this ugly human conception is not of God.

The doctrine of an everlasting hell—what does it teach ?

It teaches a place, or condition, of never-ending suffering and woe, into which all persons, unsaved at death, will pass either at once, or after a period of fearful anticipation; and that in that condition their misery will be of such a character that no earthly mental or physical tortures, however intense, can possibly be compared with it.

I have no wish to misrepresent the supporters of this doctrine, and so I will give one or two of the published statements of men who voiced the teaching of the Christian schools of thought to which they severally belonged.

The extracts following are from the writings of a Roman Catholic, a leading Anglican, and a distinguished Dissenting preacher.

They are but samples of hundreds of other statements of the same character. They show that
these representative men were on this particular
point in perfect agreement, however divergent on
other points.

The Romanist, the High-Churchman and the Bap-
tist are seen to be in fellowship in a theory of horror.

The first extract is from a work, entitled, " *The
Sight of Hell*," by Rev. J. Furniss, C. S. S. R.,
Permissu Superiorum. (The name of the author is
suggestive.)

" Little child, if you go to hell, there will be a
devil at your side to strike you. He will go on
striking you every minute *forever and ever* without
stopping. The first stroke will make your body as
bad as the body of Job, covered from head to foot
with sores and ulcers. The second stroke will
make your body twice as bad as the body of Job.
The third stroke will make your body three times
as bad as the body of Job. The fourth stroke will
make your body four times as bad as the body of
Job. How, then, will your body be, after the devil
has been striking it every moment, for a hundred

million of years without stopping? Perhaps, at this moment, seven o'clock in the evening, a child is just going into hell. To-morrow evening, at seven o'clock, go and knock at the gates of hell, and ask what the child is doing. The devils will go and look. They will come back again and say —'*The child is burning.* Go in a week and ask what the child is doing. You will get the same answer—'*It is burning.*' Go in a year and ask. The same answer comes—'*It is burning.*' Go in a million of years, and ask the same question. The answer is just the same—'*It is burning.*' So, if you go forever and ever, you will always get the same answer—'*It is burning in the fire.*'"

I make but one comment. Is it any wonder that intelligent and humane men turn shudderingly away from religion, when such a brutal conception as this is set forth in the name of Christianity, and under the sanction of the authorities in a Christian Church?

The second extract is from a sermon by the Rev. E. B. Pusey, D. D., regius professor of Hebrew, and canon of Christ Church, Oxford (quoted from "*Errors and Terrors of Blind Guides*").

"Gather in one in your mind, an assembly of all those men and women from whom, whether in history or in fiction, your memory most shrinks.

"Gather in the mind all that is most loathsome, most revolting. . . . Conceive the fierce, fiery eyes of hate, spite, frenzied rage, ever fixed on thee, looking thee through and through with hate. . . . Hear those yells of blaspheming, concentrated hate, as they echo along the lurid vault of hell; every one hating every one. . . . Yet a fixedness in that state in which the hardened malignant sinner dies, involves, without any further retribution of God, *this endless misery*."

The third extract is from a sermon on the "Resurrection of the Dead," by the Rev. C. H. Spurgeon (cited by Dean Farrar in "*Mercy and Judgment*").

"When thou diest, thy soul will be tormented alone. That will be a hell for it. But at the day of Judgment, thy body will join thy soul, and then thou wilt have twin hells; thy soul sweating drops of blood, and thy body suffused with agony. In fire, exactly like that we have on earth, thy body will lie, asbestos like, forever unconsumed, all thy veins roads for the feet of pain to travel on, every nerve a string, on which the devil shall forever play his diabolical tune of hell's unutterable lament."

I will spare my reader from any more of such writing, so unutterably horrible and revolting. I have only reproduced it in order to show *what has been taught* by sincere men in the Christian Church on the subject of future punishment. The Rev. Thomas Allin, the author of an able work—"Universalism Asserted as the Hope of the Gospel"—in commenting upon the foregoing extracts, has written these pregnant words, "Awful as are these quotations, I must repeat that they give no adequate idea at all of the horrors of hell; for that which is the very sting of its terrors—their unendingness—is beyond our power really to conceive, even approximately : so totally incommensurable are the ideas of time and of eternity." In answer to the plea that many who profess to believe in everlasting suffering no longer believe in a *material*

hell, Mr. Allin forcibly adds—" That plea, in mitigation of the horror the doctrine inspires, cannot be
admitted; for when you offer for acceptance a
spiritual, rather than a material, flame, who is there
that cannot see that the real difficulty is the same,
whether you suppose man's body burned, or his
spirit tortured ? It may even be maintained fairly,
that a hell which torments the higher part is rather
an aggravated than a mitigated penalty."

How came this doctrine to be engrafted on
Christian teaching ?

Primarily, by the mistranslation of a few Greek
words. With that we shall deal later. Secondarily,
by the influence of the Roman character upon
Christian thought and ideas.

The doctrine of an everlasting hell is an error that
must be traced to the Latin, or Western Church,
and it is from that source it has been handed down
to us. It is not a characteristic of the theology of
the Eastern Schools of Christianity during the first
three or four centuries after our Lord.

No contrast could be more remarkable than that
presented in the writings of the fathers of the early

Eastern Church and in those of the fathers of the later Western Church.

The works of the Eastern fathers are full of glowing ideas as to the universal *Fatherhood* of God; the *corrective* character of divine judgment; the complete fulfilment of the mission of Christ as the Saviour of *the world;* His triumph over all evil, and the ultimate "restitution of *all* things" to God. To them the thought appeared intolerable, that evil could be so powerful as to last forever; and God so less than omnipotent as not to be able to accomplish His purposes of mercy; and Christ's work to be so restricted that only a few of the creatures for whom He died will ever be saved. The writings of the Western fathers, on the other hand, from the time that North-African theology was grafted on the Roman stock, and became the parent of Latin Christianity, have not only set forth a pessimistic and attenuated "Gospel," but have tacked on to it the awful doctrine of everlasting woe. From the time of Augustine, until now, this dogma has lain as an incubus upon Western theology. The reformation cleansed Western Christendom of many doctrinal errors, but it left the worst of them all untouched. Protestant churches and sects, so loud in their denunciation of the Church of Rome for praying for the departed, which practice accords with the spirit of Christ, have found no difficulty in agreeing with that Church in unquestioningly accepting a doctrine which is directly opposite to His spirit.

The two theologies—that of the East and that of the West—are as wide apart as the poles. The difference between them finds an illustration in the creeds. The two great authoritative creeds of Christendom (the Apostles' and the Nicene) are Eastern, and they end with the words—"the life everlasting"—"the life of the world to come."

There is not a word in them that even hints at the doctrine of everlasting hell. The so-called Athanasian Creed, which is not Eastern, but Western, significantly closes with the words—"everlasting fire."

Happily for the cause of Christ in this twentieth century, there is a growing tendency on the part of

thoughtful Christians to look behind the teaching
of Western Christendom to the brighter and more
hopeful teaching of the early Eastern Church, near-
est in time and spirit to the Apostolic age !

The introduction of the doctrine we are considering into Christian teaching is, undoubtedly, to be
traced to the fact that Christian thought and character were influenced and lowered by coming into
contact with the Latin nation. The instincts of the
Romans were hard, exclusive, warlike and cruel.
They were a race, stolid, self-satisfied, self-centred,
haughty and pitiless. They had schooled themselves by centuries of wars, gladiatorial contests
and other degrading and brutal public spectacles, to
set a small value on human life, and to view with
complacency bloodshed and physical torture. Human agony was a leading characteristic of their
most popular pastimes.

For a while, the character of the Roman race had
little or no deteriorating influence upon Christian
thought. Christianity came to Rome with a teaching and disposition alien to Roman instincts. By
persecution after persecution, that nation heaped

upon the followers of Jesus every conceivable in-
justice and barbarity in the name of the civil power.

During that time, Christianity in its ideas contracted no contamination from the Roman
world.

But the times changed. In A. D. 324, the Roman
Emperor Constantine publicly professed the religion
of Christ, and by an Imperial edict constituted it
the religion of the state.

Hundreds of thousands of Romans, from motives
of policy and expediency only, embraced the new
religion; and became Christians in name, *without
divesting themselves of their old character and
racial instincts.*

It is not difficult to see that in these circumstances
was found a congenial soil for the growth of a
cruel and relentless doctrine.

A few fiery and enthusiastic leaders in the newly-
established Church, possessing but an imperfect
knowledge of the Greek language, and with their
old instincts as yet uneradicated, found relief and
satisfaction, under a sense of wrong done to their
Church by unbelievers and heretics, in the thought

that an awful and everlasting Divine vengeance was in store for all such offenders.

Many of the passages in the New Testament writings, grievously misunderstood, and interpreted in the light of their own instincts, appeared to favor their ideas; and thus it became possible for them to think of God as being as indifferent and pitiless in regard to human suffering as they themselves had been.

It is an illustration of the truth, that man, in his thoughts, "fashions God according to himself."

Thus only, it seems to me, is it possible to find an explanation for the fact that a great Church has been able to accept a doctrine stamped with the characteristics of old Roman cruelty and pitilessness. We believe that under no influence, except the demoralizing one of this doctrine of unending pain, conceived and born from the character of the Latin race, would it ever have been possible for a religion, bearing the name of Christ, to be associated with the Inquisition, the Smithfield fires, the burning of Servetus, and the persecution of the Quakers in America by the Puritans.

Roman hardness, cruelty, and indifference to suffering had become embodied in Western theology.

Yes, and this is not only so in respect to the doctrine we are considering. It is true of other dogmas that have disfigured Western Christianity— *e. g.*, Predestination and Reprobation.

In no Church, except in one that had suffered the influence of Latin self-consciousness, pride, exclusiveness and pitilessness, would such dogmas ever have found acceptance.

Every thoughtful Anglican ought to be devoutly thankful that the Church of England, although of Western origin, exhibits throughout her Prayer-Book so little, comparatively, of the narrow theology of the West, and so much that reflects the brighter and more hopeful teaching of the East.

We are proud of being a member of a Church that teaches us in her Litany to pray that God will "have mercy upon *all* men"; and that deliberately, in A. D., 1562, *expunged* from the Articles of Religion, one which had condemned the belief that *all* men would finally be saved.

The foundation upon which the doctrine of Everlasting Punishment has been built.

We must look for this in the mistranslation of a few words in the Greek New Testament. These words are:—αἰών (aion); αἰώνιος (aionios); κρίμα (krima); κρίσις (krisis); κρίνειν (krinein); and κατακρίνειν (katakrinein).

We shall show that the translators have dealt most misleadingly and inconsistently with these words. They have translated them, in a number of passages of Scripture in which they appear, strictly in accordance with their true meanings; while into the words as they occur in other passages they have imported meanings not only exaggerated and awful, but such as to make Scripture contradictory of itself.

For the substantiation of this serious charge, we refer the reader to the following *facts* concerning each of the words instanced.

(a) The word αἰών (aion), and the adjective derived from it, αἰώνιος (aionios).

We place these words first, because they are the terms that have been rendered by the translators—

"world without end," "forever and ever," "ever-lasting," and "eternal"; and it is upon the basis of these false renderings that the terrible doctrine of everlasting punishment has been reared.

The word αἰών, in the singular, denotes an age, a period of indefinite, but *limited*, duration, which may be either long or short. In the plural, the word denotes ages, or periods, that may be extended, and even vast, but still of *limited* duration.

The word cannot denote unendingness, commonly, but erroneously, termed "eternity," by those who forget that eternity is without beginning as well as without end. Else, how could the plural of the word be used, and how could Scripture speak of "the aions" and "the aions of the aions" (*i. e.*, "the ages," and "the ages of the ages")? There can be no plural to "eternity," and it is surely an absurdity to talk about "the eternities" and "the eternities of the eternities." And yet the translators, in some instances have deliberately imported into the world αἰών the meaning of *everlastingness*, while excluding it in other instances.

Here is an example, out of many.

In Mark iii. 29, the passage, according to the Greek, is: "He that shall blaspheme against the Holy Spirit hath not forgiveness all through the *aion* (age), but is in danger of *aionial* judgment (*i. e.,* the judgment of an age)."

The translators have rendered this: "He that shall blaspheme against the Holy Ghost hath *never* forgiveness (*i. e.,* not forgiveness *forever*), but is in danger of *eternal* damnation."

In this case, it will be seen that they have imported the idea of *unendingness* into the word αἰών, and the idea of "*eternal*" into its adjective, αἰώνιος.

In Matthew xiii. 39, the passage, according to the Greek is: "The harvest is the end of the *aion* (age)"; and in 2 Tim. iv. 10: "Demas hath forsaken me, having loved the present *aion* (age)."

The translators have rendered these passages: "The harvest is the end of the *world*." "Demas hath forsaken me, having loved this present *world*." In these cases, it will be seen that they have rightly excluded the idea of *unendingness* from the word αἰών. But why? we ask. If it was right to include it in Mark iii. 29, it was wrong to exclude it in the two last-named passages. Then why exclude it? The answer is, that it would have been too utterly foolish to translate Matthew xiii. 39, as "The harvest is the end of the *forever*," and 2 Tim. iv. 10, as "Demas hath forsaken me, having loved the present *eternity*"—and so the translators in these instances gave the word its true signification.

But can it, we ask, be right to treat language in this way—to make a word mean one thing to serve the purposes of a doctrinal idea, and to make it mean something essentially opposite, when that idea is not involved? Does any one imagine that the translators would have introduced this contradiction, and have translated the Greek of Mark xiii. 29, as they have done, unless they had gone to this text with the preconceived idea that a certain sin can never be forgiven, and therefore that the passage must be strained and contorted to endorse the idea? It is an instance, not of founding theology upon Scripture, but of twisting Scripture to suit theology. One thing is quite certain. It cannot be right to translate a word in some passages in one sense, and to translate it in other passages in an antagonistic sense. The word αἰών cannot denote a period of *limitation*, and also *unendingness*. If it denotes the one, it does not denote the other. The one definition excludes the other. No one, in his senses, dreams of defining a day as a period of twelve hours under one set of circumstances, and also as being the equivalent of *all* time under other circumstances. We have to determine what is the true definition of αἰών. If it can be shown that the essential meaning of the word is that of *limited* duration, then the case is very clear: the translators were not justified in foisting into it the idea of unendingness; and this being so, a huge superstructure of doctrine, reared upon the mistranslation, will totter and fall, and an awful nightmare will be lifted from the Christian religion. We shall the better understand the true meaning of the word αἰών by considering.

The word αἰώνιος (aionios).

Being a derivative from αἰών—an adjective of the word—it cannot denote more than the word to which it owes its origin denotes. Manifestly, it is wrong to attach to it the meaning of "everlasting" and "eternal," if the word from which it comes will not sustain the sense of unendingness, or eternity. We do not define "day-long" as that which characterizes a year, or "year-long" as that which indicates the duration of a century. Let us be consistent. The word αἰών, in the Bible, or elsewhere, never denotes endlessness, but always an age, which however long, is terminable. In spite of the liberties which the translators have taken with this word, in rendering it "forever," they have never had the presumption to render it as "eternity"; and yet over and over again they have translated its adjective—αἰώνιος—as "*eternal*." Is this consistent? we ask. Must there not be something radically faulty in the system (or want of system) of interpretation, which affixes to the word αἰών the meaning of "*world*" in such passages as Matt. xiii. 39, 40, 49; xxiv. 3; Mark iv. 19; Luke i. 70; xvi. 8; xx. 34; John ix. 32; Acts iii. 21; xv. 18; and in many others; and then affixes the meaning of "*everlasting*" or "*eternal*" to its adjective, αἰώνιος, in Matt. xviii. 8; xxv. 41, 46; Mark iii. 29; Luke xvi. 9; John iii. 15; and in scores of similar passages.

An adjective qualifies its noun, and we cannot import into the adjective *more* than is contained in the noun. We may speak of the race of mankind as "humanity," and describe the existence of the race as "human life," but we should not be so absurd as to define "human" in that phrase as signifying "Divine."

And yet the translators have been guilty of committing a similar error in translating the word αἰών in the passages instanced as "world," which is equivalent to an age, and expresses limitation; while translating αἰώνιος as "everlasting" and "eternal"; both of which terms exclude limitation.

We ask, does this commend itself as being a fair way of dealing with a book which contains a record of Divine truth?

It will help us considerably in arriving at the true meaning of the words αἰών and αἰώνιος, if we turn to the Septuagint, and notice their significance as they are used there. Most of my readers know that the Septuagint is the Greek Version of the Old Testament in use among the Jews in the time of our Lord.

Do the words as there used convey the sense of unendingness ? On the contrary, they are applied to things and circumstances that have long since *ceased to exist.*

For example, in Gen. xiii. 15, God is represented as saying to Abram—"All the land which thou seest, to thee will I give it and to thy seed *so long as an age* (ἑώς αἰῶνος)."

How have the translators dealt with this ? Into the word αἰών they have imported the meaning of unendingness, and made the passage read—" To thee will I give it and to thy seed *forever.*"

A tremendous difference, surely ! In other words, they imply by their mistranslation that God has not kept His promise. The land of Canaan does not now belong to the descendants of Abraham, nor has it been in their possession for very many centuries.

Again, in Num. xxv. 13, God promises to Phineas, the grandson of Aaron, and to his seed after him an *age-long* (αἰωνία) covenant of priest-hood.

What have the translators done here? They have imported the sense of "everlasting" into the word αἰώνιος, and again represented God as being unfaithful. The Aaronic priesthood was not an *everlasting* one. The office has long ago ceased, and if the Christian religion is true it will never be revived.

Again, in Joshua xiv. 9, Caleb is most solemnly promised that certain land in Palestine shall be his and his children's for *an age* (αἰῶνα).

How has this passage been treated by the trans-lators? Just in the same way. An exaggerated meaning has been thrust into αἰών, and the state-ment has been made untrue, by their rendering the passage—"Thine inheritance and thy children's *forever.*" Neither that part nor any other part of Palestine has belonged to Caleb's descendants for dozens of centuries.

I could multiply instances such as these, but will take but one more.

In Psalm xxiv. 7, 9, the splendid Temple once at

Jerusalem is referred to in the words—"Lift up your heads, O ye gates, and be ye lifted up, ye *age-lasting* (αἰώνιοι) doors." The passage is sensible enough as it stands in the original and in the Septuagint; but it expresses an untruth as the translators have rendered it—"ye *everlasting* doors." What! the doors of the Temple everlasting! when it is an historical fact that that Temple was burnt and razed to the ground ages ago.

In the Revised Version of the Bible, the translators evidently saw the inconsistency of describing as "*everlasting*" the doors of a building that no longer exists, and so they have given "*ancient*" as a marginal reading. But why do that, and at the same time leave standing the words "forever," in Gen. xiii. 15, and Joshua xiv. 9, and "everlasting" in Numbers xxv. 13? Is this consistent? we ask again. The Greek word is the same in all these passages. If αἰώνιος can be rendered "ancient," it certainly cannot be correctly rendered "everlasting." Everlastingness is *not* implied by the word "ancient"; and therefore we are very grateful to the revisers for having admitted by their marginal note that αἰώνιος may mean something very different from "everlasting." In Deut. xxiii. 3, is a passage which ought to have been sufficient to open the eyes of the translators as to the real meaning of αἰών.—An Ammonite or Moabite shall not enter into the congregation of the Lord; even to their *tenth generation* shall they not enter into the congregation of the Lord for *the aion* (*i. e.*, the age, or epoch).

Here the *aion* is actually defined as being equivalent to a period of ten generations, and the translators by rendering it as "forever," have committed themselves to the astounding statement that ten generations constitute unendingness. We could smile at this inconsistency and inaccuracy, did we not know that it is from such that a monstrous doctrine has arisen, which has overshadowed and oppressed for centuries the religion of Jesus.

What sort of assurance can we have of the truthfulness of the dogma of unending punishment, when we know that these two Greek words, αἰών and αἰώνιος, have been juggled with in passages of Scripture supposed to support that dogma, in precisely the same way as in the passages just adduced;

and that the words "everlasting," and "eternal"—
of such awful and appalling import when placed
before "fire," "judgment" and "damnation," etc.
—are only mistranslations of the word αἰώνιος (age
long)—a word that has been applied to a host of
things that have no existence now!

We pass on to the brief consideration of a few
other words that have been dealt with unfairly, in
order, if not to found, at all events to buttress, this
doctrine of everlasting punishment.

(*b*)   The word κρίμα (krima)

The word denotes *judgment;* the sentence pronounced. As such the translators of the Author-
ised Version rightly rendered it in many passages
of the Gospels, the Acts, and the Epistles (*e. g.*,
Matt. vii. 2; John ix. 39; Acts xxiv. 25; and Rom.
ii. 2). But here is the inconsistency. In Matt.
xxiii. 14; Mark xii. 40; Luke xx. 47; Rom. iii. 8;
xiii. 2; 1 Cor. xi. 29; and 1 Tim. v. 12, they substituted the word "*damnation*" for it. We will say
nothing about this word "damnation," except that it
is an evil-sounding word, whose original meaning
has been exaggerated and perverted ; and a word

that more than any other has been employed to
support the awful doctrine we are opposing.

But why did the translators alter the reading?
Why render κρίμα as "judgment" in some places,
and as "damnation" in others? The answer is—
These last named passages were viewed as pointing
to future punishment; the translators' idea of
future punishment was that of endless suffering
and misery; and the word "damnation" was considered to be better suited to the popular theological
error than the proper and milder word, "judgment." Our contention is, if the word "damnation" be right in one passage, it is right in another.
Why for example—did they not translate John ix.
39, so as to represent our Lord as saying—"For
damnation (κρίμα) I came into this world"? They
gave the true rendering in this and other passages,
because it would have been too absurd not to do so.

That these criticisms are not unjustified is seen in
the fact that the New Testament revisers have discarded the word "damnation" in the above passages, and in Rom. xiii. 2 and 1 Cor. xi. 29, have
correctly rendered κρίμα as "judgment."

We are thankful to them for this service in the interests of truth.

We must briefly consider —

(c) The word κρίσις (krisis).

It also denotes *judgment, i. e.,* the process of judging; and in forty-one passages of the New Testament the translators so rendered it. But in Matt. xxiii. 33; Mark iii. 29; and John v. 29, they deliberately substituted the word "*damnation*" for "judgment." With what object? Plainly to add emphasis to their preconceived idea of an endless hell. But does this commend itself as being a fair and consistent way of dealing with Scripture?

Why,—except that it was too utterly foolish,— not have rendered the following passages as they did the three just instanced?

"Woe unto you, Scribes and Pharisees, hypocrites! for ye . . . pass over *damnation* (κρίσις) and the love of God" (Luke xi. 42).

"As I hear, I judge, and My *damnation* (κρίσις) is just" (John v. 30).

"So opened He not His mouth ; in His humiliation His *damnation* (κρίσις) was taken away " (Acts viii. 32, 33).

Seeing that the Greek word is the same in every one of these passages, is it not very wrong to give it an improper and grossly exaggerated significance in three texts, while translating it correctly in forty-one other instances ?

Again, it is suggestive that the revisers of the New Testament, in Matt. xxiii. 33 and John v. 29, have flung away the word "*damnation*," and in its place put "judgment" as the proper rendering of κρίσις. If the translators of the Authorized Version had done this, one of the supports of an ancient error would have been knocked down.

(*d*)   The word κρίνειν (krinein).

The word denotes—to *judge ;* and eighty-one times in the New Testament the translators so rendered it.   And yet in regard to the same Greek word which occurs in 2 Thess. ii. 12, they made the translation run:—"That they all might be *damned* who believed not the truth."

But why not have been consistent ?   Why not have rendered 1 Cor. vi. 2, in this way; since in both passages the verb (*κρίνειν*) is the same,—"Do ye not know that the saints shall *damn* the world? and if the world shall be *damned* by you, are ye unworthy to *damn* the smallest matters?"

I will trouble the reader with only one other word.

(*e*) The word *κατακρίνειν* (katakrinein).

Its meaning is—to *condemn*. It is a stronger word than *κρίνειν*, to judge, but there is nothing in it that corresponds to that awful meaning supposed to reside in the word "damn." And yet the translators did not hesitate to give it that meaning.

How did they treat this verb, *κατακρίνειν*? Just as they treated other verbs and nouns, when they wished to bolster their theological idea. In seventeen instances in the New Testament they translated it rightly as "*condemn*," but in Mark xvi. 16 and Rom xiv. 23, doctrinal preconceptions prevailed, and so these two passages were rendered—"He that believeth not shall be *damned*." "He that doubteth is *damned* if he eat."

And for centuries, an everlasting hell-fire has been read unto the mistranslated word.

Again we say,—Why not have been consistent,
and have translated Matt. xxvii. 3 and John viii.
10, 11 (where the verb is the same) as follows,—
"Then Judas, when he saw that He (Christ) was
damned, etc." "Hath no man *damned* thee?
. . . Neither do I *damn* thee."

We venture to say that the translators would
have rendered these passages in this way, if they
had borne any reference to punishment after death.
But can it be right to invest, in one case, a Greek
word with a certain meaning, so as to make it a
prop for a horrible doctrine, and to divest it of that
meaning, in another case, because the word when
so invested would assert too much, and reduce the
statement to absurdity?

Surely that cannot be an honest way of dealing
with Scripture. Such a method of interpretation
would not be tolerated for a moment outside the
domain of theology.

Having now considered a few of those Greek
words, upon the mistranslation of which the doctrine of everlasting punishment has been made to
rest, we are in a position to estimate the *true* signi-

fication of the words themselves, and further, to judge whether certain passages of Scripture, alleged to teach that doctrine really do so or not.

It is a principle of the Church of England, as expressed in Article VI., that whatsoever may not be proved by Holy Scripture, "is not to be required of any man that it should be believed as an article of the faith."

We claim that this doctrine is not only *not proved* by Holy Scripture, when correctly translated, but is absolutely *disproved* by it.

We have seen that the true meanings of the Greek words in question are as follows:

αἰών (aion, or æon)—an age; a period long, or short, but of *limited* duration.

αἰώνιος (aionios)—an adjective derived from αἰών, denoting, that which pertains to an aion, or æon; rightly translated by such terms as: "aionial," "age-long," or "age-lasting," which denote limitation; but wrongly translated by "everlasting," and "eternal," which exclude limitation.

κρίμα (krima)—judgment, *i. e.*, the sentence pronounced.

κρίσις (krisis)—judgment, *i. e.*, the process of judging.

κρίνειν (krinein)—to judge (not necessarily to *condemn*).

κατακρίνειν (katakrinein)—to condemn.

We now give *correct* translations of the most important of those passages in the Bible which refer to future punishment, in which one or more of these Greek words appear.

We would suggest that the reader should refer to each of the passages in the Authorized Version of the Bible, in order to better realize the vital contrast that is presented.

Passages referring to Future Punishments, as they appear in the Greek New Testament.

Matt. xviii. 8, "To be cast into the fire which is *aionial*, or *age-long* (αἰώνιος)."

Matt. xxiii. 14, "Ye shall receive a greater *judgment* (κρίμα)."

Matt. xxiii. 33, "How can ye escape the *judgment* (κρίμα) of Gehenna ?"

Matt. xxv. 46, "These shall go away into an

Appendix 241

age-long (αἰώνιος) pruning," (*i. e.*, the *remedial* discipline pertaining to an age, or æon).

Mark iii. 29, "He that shall blaspheme against the Holy Spirit hath not forgiveness all through *the age* (αἰών), but is in danger of an *age-long* (αἰώνιος) *judgment* (κρίσις)" (or an age-long *sin*, as another reading of the text gives it).

Mark xvi. 16, "He that believeth not shall be *condemned* (κατακρίνειν)."

Luke xx. 47, "The same shall receive a greater *judgment* (κρίμα)."

John v. 29, "Unto a resurrection of *judgment* (κρίσις)."

Rom. iii. 8, "Whose *judgment* (κρίμα) is just."

Rom. xiii. 2, "They that resist (the powers that be) shall receive to themselves *judgment*" (κρίμα ; *i. e.*, the judgment of the civil magistrate; not future punishment, as the translators implied by the word "damnation ").

1 Cor. xi. 29, "He that eateth and drinketh unworthily eateth and drinketh *judgment* (κρίμα) to himself."

2 Thess. i. 9, "Who shall be punished (lit. who

shall pay justice), viz., an *age-long* (αιώνιος) destruction from the presence of the Lord."

2 Thess. ii. 12, "That they all might be judged (κρίνειν) who believed not the truth."

1 Tim. v. 12, "Having *judgment* (κρίμα) because they have cast off their first faith."

Heb. vi. 2, "The doctrine of . . . an *aionial*, or *age-long*, (αἰώνιος) judgment."

2 Peter ii. 17, "To whom the gloom of darkness all through *an age* (αιών) has been reserved."

Jude 7, "Suffering the justice of an *aionial*, or *age-long*, fire."

Jude 13, "To whom the gloom of darkness all through the *age* has been reserved."

Rev. xiv. 11, "The smoke of their testing goeth up all through *ages* of *ages* (αἰών)."

Rev. xix. 3, "Her smoke goeth up all through the *ages* of the *ages* (αἰών)."

Rev. xx. 10, "They shall be tested (or tried) day and night all through the *ages* of the *ages* (αἰών)."

There are a few passages in the New Testament, which are supposed, by those who have not examined them, to especially support the doctrine of unending torment and woe.

Three of them appear in the list given above: Rev. xiv. 11; xix. 3 and xx. 10.

"Surely," says the supporter of the so-called "orthodox" dogma—"the words—'Her smoke goeth up all through the ages of the ages'—teach everlasting suffering! If the phrase—'Forever and ever'—be discarded and the words—'all through the ages of ages'—be substituted, does it not amount to the same thing—*unendingness ?*" We answer—No. It simply points to a long and indefinite, but *terminable*, period. An aion, or age, is a *terminable* period, however long it may last; and if you add any number of aions or ages together they will not represent *unendingness*, or a million-millionth fraction of it. That being so, it is illogical to account anything *everlasting*, because it may last for ages of ages.

But consider for a moment these three passages in the Revelation, to which such an immense amount of undue importance has been attached.

In the first place, they appear in a book of the

Bible, which, although ultimately admitted into the canon of Holy Scripture, was for a long time excluded from it. During the early centuries of the Christian Church, the Book of the Revelation was viewed with much suspicion, and there were many who considered that it should not be numbered among the canonical books on account of the essentially Jewish tone of thought pervading it. Certainly, it is a book wholly unlike the other books of the New Testament. It is full of extraordinary imagery, curious metaphor and hyperbole, mysterious visions, "the kabbalism of numbers and the symbolism of strange figures." To turn from the gospel and epistles of St. John to the Revelation, is (as Dr. Farrar has pointed out) to pass "from the most ethereal regions of Christian thought to scarlet dragons and hell-born frogs; from realms of spiritual assurance, in which the pure azure of contemplation seems to be unstained by any earthly cloud, to dim images of plague and war, in which cries of vengeance ring through an atmosphere which is lurid with fire and blood."

To treat a book of this character as if its utterances were the language of scientific theology is absurd, and worse than absurd. And yet this has been done. Again, why read into these three passages a *literal* interpretation, when at the same time no one would dream of doing this in regard to Isaiah xxxiv. 9, 10—the passage by which, undoubtedly, they were suggested? The prophet, in impassioned Oriental language, was describing the temporal calamities that should befall the land of Idumea. He writes (we quote from the Septuagint)—The land thereof shall become burning pitch, and it shall not be quenched, night and day, all through the age of time (lit the *aion-time ;* a phrase which the translators have taken the liberty of rendering as "*forever*").

Are we, from this statement, prepared to argue that the land of Idumea is still burning, and will continue to burn to the end of time, or forever? If not, why attach a literal meaning to figurative texts in the Book of Revelation, in order to make them props for a horrible doctrine, and not attach it to this statement of Isaiah?

Does any one imagine that the moon is literally

"turned into blood," because the writers of the Bible describe the redness of a lunar eclipse in those terms? So then, we contend that these three particular passages, taken as they stand in the original, do not give the slightest intimation of unending punishment. At most, they do but point to a prolonged, but *terminable*, judgment.

In Mark ix. 43 to 48, there occurs a passage, supposed by many to clearly support the doctrine we are opposing—"Where their worm dieth not, and the fire is not quenched."

The following is a fair representation of how the passage has been handled by commentators, credited with some knowledge of logic.

"The worm is *undying;* therefore its prey, and the pains it inflicts upon it must last *forever.* The fire, too, is unquenchable ; therefore its victim must always continue to be forever burning, although never consumed."

Sense, common sense! is all we ask for. The passage is a quotation from Isaiah lxvi. 24. The prophet had not the glimmer of an idea of "eternal torment" in his mind when he penned those words. He is referring to the valley of Hinnom—a spot outside Jerusalem—where great fires were constantly kept burning to consume the offal and refuse of the city. The undying worm was not its prey; nor was the unquenchable fire that which it consumed. The victims of both were not *living* things at all, but *dead*, insensible bodies;—the "*carcasses* of the men, the transgressed against God."

The punishment is no longer being inflicted; the worm in that valley is no longer living, and the fires, having served their purpose, have ages ago gone out. And yet, forsooth, this has been one of the principal stock-passages adduced in support of the theory of endless suffering.

What our Lord intended to teach, when He quoted this text from Isaiah, was, that there is in the universe of God a principle—symbolized by the worm and the fire—which will remove and consume all that is corrupt and worthless ; that this principle is an undying one; and that no soul can escape the action of this principle until the last vestige of dross in him shall have disappeared, and the evil in his nature shall have been consumed. "*Every one*" (not some only) said Jesus, in connection with this particular passage, "shall be salted with fire" (Mark ix. 49).

We ask which is the more reasonable interpretation of this text; that, as we have given it, or that which, in a futile attempt to make the passage fit in with a theological preconception, confounds the *agent* with the *object* of judgment, and views the man as if he were the same as the worm and the fire.

Matt. xxvi. 24, and the corresponding verse in Mark xiv. 21, "Woe unto that man by whom the Son of Man is betrayed! *It had been good for that man if he had not been born*"—has been so dealt with by the translators as to make it appear a prop for the doctrine of irremedial punishment in the world beyond. By confusing the pronouns—that which refers to our Lord, and that which refers to Judas,—and by substituting the words "*that man*" for "*Him*," they have made the passage read as if it were a declaration that Judas was hopelessly and finally lost.

Christ did not say that it had been a good thing
for *Judas*, if Judas had not been born; but that it
would have been a good thing for Himself, from
His standpoint as the Son of Man,—if His betrayer
had not been born.   An ingredient in the Saviour's
cup of bitterness would not have been there.

We give the words as they stand in the Greek of
both passages and leave the reader to draw his own
inference.

"The Son of Man goeth, as it has been written
concerning Him (αὐτοῦ, *i. e.*, the Son of Man): but
woe to that man (ἐκείνω, *i. e.*, Judas) through whom
the Son of Man is betrayed!   A good thing were it
for Him (αὐτῷ, *i. e.*, the Son of Man, not Judas) if
that man (ἐκεῖνος, *i. e.*, Judas) had not been born."

The pronoun αὐτός refers to Christ, and the pronoun ἐκεῖνος to Judas.

Thus, from our examination of the foregoing
passages which have formed the basis of the doctrine of unending suffering, we see that not one of
them is capable of sustaining the strain placed upon
them.   Strip these few Greek words of the false
and exaggerated meanings arbitrarily imported into

them, and these passages not only negative the doctrine we have mentioned, but point to an absolutely opposite conclusion, viz. :—*That all future punishments are fatherly, remedial aud terminable.*

Let us, in as few words as possible, try to grasp the glorious truth expressed in this statement. Manifestly, we cannot believe that God's judgments are remedial—*i. e.*, that they are means for the recovery of sinners—without enlarging our ideas as to God Himself, and as to the character and scope of His great purpose of salvation.

If we believe that, after some future æon of judgment and discipline, sinners, humbled and repentant, will find their way back to God, then, necessarily, we shall discard the popular notion that the great Father will save only a few comparatively out of earth's teeming millions; and we shall not believe that this earth-life, this æon of time, is the only period in which He will work out His beneficent purpose.

What do we gather from Scripture on this subject of God's great purpose of salvation?

First, that it is a purpose, the working out of

which is not restricted to this world-æon, or age, or to any of those "æon-times" (as St. Paul calls them in 2 Tim. i. 9), which come within the compass of this world's history, and are called by us "dispensations"; but that it is a purpose that will continue to be worked out in æons or ages *after* the present world-æon shall have ceased to exist.

Accordingly, St. Paul in Eph. iii. 11, describes it as God's "Purpose *of the æons*." The translators obscured the meaning of this passage, by treating the noun in it as if it were an adjective, and making it read "*eternal* purpose."

Now, when we turn to the Greek New Testament, we find that in speaking of the redeeming plan of God a constant reference is made to these "æons"—these succeeding and limitable ages or epochs

St. Paul, in speaking of God's "Purpose of the æons," makes two statements respecting it.

He declares, that as regards its conception it is antecedent to this world-æon, with its dispensations, or æon-times; and moreover that in scope and operation it extends beyond it.

That purpose of salvation he asserts, in 1 Cor. ii. 7, was ordained "*before the æons* unto our glory." In Eph. iii. 9, 10, 21, he refers to it as a mystery hidden in God from the æons, although now made known; and declares that a glory will accrue to God from it "*through all the generations of the æon of the æons.*"

This latter phrase is a very remarkable one. The translators evidently did not perceive its meaning and so rendered the passage—"throughout all ages, world without end." But again we must point out that such a rendering is a contradiction in terms. An age is a *limitable* period, and no number of ages can be the equivalent of "world *without end.*" We might just as well say—"Throughout all the days of one particular month of the months, year without end."

There is no difficulty at all in this phrase of St. Paul—"Through all the generations of the æon of the æons." The apostle clearly intimates that there is one vast epoch, which he calls "*the æon* of the æons," so vast that its generations cover the whole course of time, as well as æons after this world-

æon,—and that during this epoch the "Purpose of
the æons," *i. e.*, the redemption of the whole human race, will be worked out to the glory of God.

The popular idea is, that when the end of this
world shall come, all ages and dispensations will
cease, and eternity begin.

The Scripture most certainly does not teach this.
It asserts that there will be *limitable* ages beyond
this present world age. In Eph. i. 21, Christ is said
to be set "far above all principality and power
. . . not only in *this æon*, but also in that (an
æon) *which is to come.*" Here, at all events, the
idea is negatived that the end of this age is the end
of all ages.

In Eph. ii. 4–7, St. Paul affirms that God's display
of love and mercy towards us was for a particular
purpose, viz., "that in *the æons to come* He might
shew the exceeding riches of His grace towards us."

There is no sense in speaking of "æons to come,"
if this æon is the last of limitable periods, and all
beyond is that illimitable duration, unmarked by
time and epochs—viz., everlastingness.

Then again we gather from Scripture, rightly

translated, that our Lord's work of saving souls will not cease when this world-age and its dispensations shall terminate.

In Heb. xiii. 8, Christ is declared to be the "*same*, yesterday, and to-day, and *all through the æons.*" We know what He was in the past—a Saviour. We know what He is to-day—the same. Will He not be a Saviour all through those æons? If not, He is other than He was and is, and consequently the statement regarding Him is untrue.

Moreover, in Rev. i. 8, our Lord Himself is represented as saying—"Behold, I am living *all through* the æons of the æons; and have the keys of Hades and of death." We ask—Did He mean by this that He, "the Saviour of all men," would merely act as the jailor of ruined souls; or did He mean that all through those æons of the æons His saving work would be continued, and that He would open the doors of Hades and death to set the prisoners, after their remedial discipline, free?

One thing is very certain. The latter supposition is in harmony with the assertion that He will be "the same" all through the ages as He

was and is. The jailor-theory does not agree
with it.

Further, scripture also distinctly teaches that all
the æons are no more than *limitable* periods; inasmuch as it asserts that they will come to an end.
In 1 Cor. xv. 24, St. Paul writes—"Then (or afterwards) *cometh the end*" (*i. e.*, the end of all these
æons); when with death and every other enemy
overcome, and with *all* things (not *some* only) sub-
dued unto Christ, Christ Himself shall deliver up the
kingdom to God "so that God may be all in *all*"
(v. 28).

What do we gather from the foregoing, and
from a great deal more in the Bible of the same
character? That God's grand purpose of saving
the human race is a beneficent scheme, whose
working is not restricted (as some have thought) to
a moment of duration—the earth-life, in the case of
individuals; or to a world-age, in the case of the
race of mankind; but that it is a purpose whose
accomplishment will be worked out in ages yet to
come.

God's intentions of goodness and mercy towards

individual man will not disappear when he shall have lived out his little span of earthly existence; nor will the destiny of the race have been fulfilled, when this planet shall have ceased to be the abode of human life, and the world æon shall be no more.

Man was made to live on, and so was God's grand purpose of salvation in regard to him.

This age will close, and still the purpose of God towards the race will be unaccomplished. Another age will dawn. It will start with a manifestation of Christ from the spiritual world. During that epoch of Christ-manifestation the purpose of God will work on. Christ's faithful servants will commence a dispensation of dignity and service for others as "the Bride of the Lamb," and the "foolish virgins" will be shut out of that dignity and service; but not to be "damned for all eternity," as some tract-writers say. Still, the purpose of God towards the race will be unaccomplished. Another age will dawn—an age of perfecting for some; an age of judgment, of painful disciplining and pruning, and of awakening, for others.

That age, too, will have its end; and the Christ,

amid all these changes, will remain unchangeable—
the same as of old, the *saving* One.

Another and, perhaps, another age will dawn and
close, and still the great Father of love will be found
to be working out His great project of love.

And so on, and so on, until the last of the æons
shall have run its course; and then—"*then cometh
the end*," when the magnificent purpose of God
shall have been achieved, and He shall be "all
things in *all men.*"

Has not Scripture called God's plan of redemption
—"the Purpose *of the ages?*"

When we have grasped the truth expressed above,
how significant become such passages as these—
Heb. v. 9, "*æonian* salvation," *i. e.*, the salvation
of the ages; Heb. ix. 12, "*æonian* redemption,"
i. e., the redemption of the ages; Heb. xiii. 20, "the
æonian covenant," *i. e.*, the covenant pertaining to
the ages during which the purpose of God will be
worked out. The adjective in all three of these
passages is the same—αἰώνιος, and yet in two instances the translators rendered it as "eternal," and
in one instance as "everlasting."

In enlarging our ideas, therefore, as to the periods through which God's purpose of salvation will be worked out, we take the first step towards realizing the true character of future punishments. They are not vindictive and endless; but remedial and terminable. They are not monuments of perpetuated evil, but instruments in the hands of God for good.

There will be a disciplinary fire which is age long (Matt. xviii. 8); there will be a painful "pruning" which is age-long (Matt. xxv. 46); there will be a "judgment" which is age-long (Mark iii. 29); and a "destruction from the presence of the Lord" which is age-long (2 Thess. i. 9); and a "gloom of darkness" for impenitent sinners all through an age (2 Pet. ii. 17); but all these things are the characteristics *only of an age*. The purpose of God will outlive and work through the epoch of judgment, because it is a purpose not of one æon, but "of the æons." Yes, and it is a purpose that contemplates *salvation*, not ruin.

We pass on to consider another very important point in regard to God's "Purpose of the ages."

Secondly. God's purpose of saving mankind is

declared by Scripture to embrace the *whole* and not merely a *part* of the human race.

The early Eastern Church grasped this magnificent gospel-truth; but the later Western Church, after coming into contact with the proud and exclusive Latin nation, failed to do so.

The mental attitude of a great number of Christians, in regard to the purpose of God, is as illogical as it is possible for it to be. They will start by most solemnly assuring you that they accept certain statements of the Bible as the words of truth, and end by professing their belief in a doctrine of future punishment, which flatly contradicts every one of those statements.

Take an illustration of what I mean. Ask any of those Christians who do not accept the "larger hope"—"Do you believe the following passages?"

"God was in Christ, reconciling *the world* unto Himself" (2 Cor. v. 19).

God sent His Son, "that *the world* through Him *might be saved*" (John iii. 17).

"I, if I be lifted up from the earth, will draw *all* men unto Me" (John xii. 32).

"God our Saviour, who willeth that *all men* should *be saved*" (1 Tim. ii. 3, 4).

"God—who is *the Saviour of all men*, specially of those that believe" (1 Tim. iv. 10).

The answer will be—"Most certainly; we account them Divinely inspired utterances."

"Do you, then, acknowledge that one day God will have completely triumphed over all sin and evil, that the *whole* race of mankind will have been brought into union with Himself through the saving work of Christ?"

"Oh! dear no," is replied. "We view that as a dreadfully heretical notion. It would do away with hell and punishment." "Precisely so," we answer, "and that is exactly what these passages declare: viz., that hell and punishment, when they shall have served their purpose, will one day disappear from the universe of God, because ultimately the Christ will draw *all* men, and God the Saviour, will save *all.*"

We see, therefore, the illogical manner in which these passages are treated: they are read and interpreted as if the words we have italicized were not

in them at all. They are explained in such a way
that the reader must understand that the word
"*world*" only means "*part* of the world" and the
word "*all*" signifies no more than "*some.*" In
other words—not one of these passages is true, if
future punishment be either everlasting or irremedial. If, at the great consummation—"the restitution of *all* things" (Acts iii. 21), a hundred souls,
or even one soul, be finally and irretrievably lost, it
will not be a fact that the crucified Lord will have
drawn *all* men unto Himself, nor will it be true that
God is "the *Saviour* of *all* men." Now, there is a
whole host of passages—hundreds of them—in the
Bible, similar to those just adduced. They all emphatically declare that God's purpose of saving mankind will embrace not merely a *part* of the race,
but the *whole* of it. How have these passages been
treated by the majority of Christian teachers? Practically, as if they had had no existence. Their plain,
unequivocal, affirmative declarations as to the *universal* scope of God's redemptive plan have been
quietly ignored, and a theory of future punishment
has been propounded of such a character that no

one can accept it without first rejecting the declarations of those passages. We ask the reader to forget for a moment all he has been taught; to read the following passages of Scripture; and then to honestly ask himself—What do they teach?

"Unto Thee shall *all flesh* come" (Ps. lxv. 2).

"I have sworn by Myself . . . That unto Me *every* knee shall bow, *every* tongue shall swear" (Is. xlv. 23).

"He shall see of the travail of His soul, and *shall be satisfied*" (Is. liii. 11).

"And it shall come to pass afterwards, that I will pour out My spirit upon *all* flesh" (Joel ii. 28).

"The son of man came *to save that which is lost*" (Matt. xviii. 11).

"All flesh *shall* see the *salvation* of God" (Luke iii. 6).

"And go after that which is lost, *until he find it*" (Luke xv. 4).

"The Lamb of God which taketh away the sin of *the world*" (John i. 29).

"The Father loveth the Son, and hath given *all things* into His hand. . . . And this is the

Father's will which hath sent Me, that of *all* which He hath given Me *I should lose nothing*" (John iii. 35; vi. 39).

"I came not to judge the world, but *to save the world*" (John xii. 47).

"The times of restitution of *all* things" (Acts iii. 21).

"For God hath concluded them all in unbelief, that He might have mercy upon *all*" (Rom. xi. 32).

"For of Him, and through Him, and *unto Him* are *all* things" (Rom. xi. 36).

"As I live, saith the Lord, *every* knee shall bow to Me, and *every* tongue shall confess to God" (Rom. xiv. 11).

"As in Adam all die, even so in Christ shall *all* be made alive" (1 Cor. xv. 22).

"That God may be all in *all*" (1 Cor. xv. 28).

"That in the dispensation of the completing of the times, He might gather together in one *all* things in Christ, both which are in the heavens, and which are on the earth; even in Him" (Eph. i. 10).

"According to the working whereby He is able

even to subdue *all* things unto Himself " (Phil. iii. 21).

"By Him (Christ) to reconcile *all* things unto Himself; by Him, whether they be things on the earth, or whether they be things in the heavens " (Col. i. 20).

"God our Saviour, who willeth that *all men should be saved*" (1 Tim. ii. 3, 4).

"Who (Christ) gave Himself a ransom for *all;* the testimony (of this) to be borne in its own times" (1 Tim. ii. 6).

"The Lord is . . . not willing that any should perish, but that *all should advance unto repentance*" (2 Pet. iii. 9).

"He is the propitiation for our sins; and not for ours only, but also for the sins of *the whole world*" (1 John ii. 2).

"The Father sent the Son, *the Saviour of the world*" (1 John iv. 14).

To this list we could add scores and scores of passages both from the Old and New Testaments, all of the same purport. What do they mean; what do they teach? Do they not affirm, as plainly and emphatically as any words can possibly do, the magnificent truth which was preached by Christ and apostles, viz., that God's saving of mankind will not be a saving of merely a *part* of the race, but of the *whole* of it?

Those passages tell us that, when God's great "Purpose of the ages" shall have been worked out, He will be what every good and thoughtful mind would wish He should be—the conqueror of evil; the focus of the love and devotion of His creature man; the "all in *all*."

And it is upon this truth, so plainly declared in the pages of Scripture, that we ground our belief that all the future punishments of God are fatherly, remedial, and terminable. If the final outcome of God's purpose is—as the Bible declares—the salvation of *all*, then it must follow that no judgment nor punishment, be it ever so prolonged or ever so painful, can be anything else than a discipline of mercy; a means to an end, and that end—good.

A thousand and one difficulties confront those who contend that future punishments are *not* fatherly, remedial and terminable. How, for instance, can they answer such questions as follows :

(*a*) Christ is to see of the travail of His soul and to be satisfied. Will He be *satisfied*, if numbers of those whom He loved, and for whom He died, shall be finally and irretrievably lost ? If at the end there shall be but *one* wretched straggler who has not been found, do they think He will be *satisfied?* He will not be, if He meant what He said about going after lost sheep.

(*b*) God has declared that by Christ He will reconcile *all* things unto Himself. If any at the last shall be irrecoverably lost, those souls will *not* have been reconciled. Will God, then, not do that which He declares it is His will to do? Is this, we ask, compatible with any idea of sovereign will ?

(*c*) God, it is declared, shall be, when the end cometh, "all in *all*." Will those who differ from us explain how this can possibly be, if any, or even one, of the human race be ever finally, hopelessly and everlastingly ruined and lost ?

Lastly. There are passages in the Bible that distinctly affirm that future punishments will *not* be irremedial and unending.

In Ps. ciii. 9, "He will not always chide; neither will He keep His anger all through the age (αἰών)." In Ps. cxxxvi. there are 26 verses which refer to various judgments of God on sinners, and each verse ends with the words:—"For His mercy endureth all through the age (αἰών)."

In Ps. lvii. 16, "For I will not contend all through the age (αἰών), neither will I be always wroth; for the spirit should fail before Me, the souls which I have made."

In Jer. iii. 12, "I will not keep anger all through the age (αἰών)."

In Lam. iii. 31, "The Lord will not cast off all through the age (αἰών)."

The translators rendered this phrase—"all through the age" (which is as it stands in the Septuagint)—by the words "*forever*", thereby strengthening the case against themselves. Where is the sense in saying in one breath that God will *not* keep His anger or cast off *forever*, and in asserting in the next breath that His wrath and judgments and punishments are *everlasting?* They have made Scripture self-contradictory.

On the other hand, there is no contradiction, and a beautiful Gospel-truth comes into view, if the word " αἰών " be translated rightly.

" His mercy endureth all through *the age.*"

" The Lord will not cast off all through *the age.*"

What age? Why, the age of judgment, punishment and pruning. But the mercy of God will not fail during it; His anger will not be kept throughout it; the age will run its course, but it will not involve His casting off of souls whom He judges and prunes. Yes, and is not this exactly what we should expect in regard to a Heavenly Father, concerning whom Jesus said that, " To such an extent He loved the world "?

He is "Love"; He is better and nobler than any good, but imperfectly loving, earthly father can be. We who are good fathers can be angry with our sons for their wrong-doing, and we may inflict upon them—and rightly too—a severe, and, if the case demand it, even prolonged punishment for their welfare. For weeks, or months, or more, our wilful boy may be made to suffer the disciplining of our love and concern for him.

But does our righteous anger not abate; do we cast off and disown the boy, during that period of discipline? Nay, not if we be true fathers.

For the boy's good, we make the discipline last until the purpose of fatherly love be accomplished; but the anger is gone. By the punishment we inflict, we may suffer more than the lad himself.

For his good, not a whit of that punishment can we remit; but he is no castaway because of that. Is the great Father as good as we are?

Oh! read this thought into the verses instanced above, and how luminous, how gloriously pregnant with Divine meaning, they become!

We turn to other passages. In Matt. v. 26, our Lord in referring to future punishment as "a prison," asserts, " Thou shalt by no means come out thence, *till* thou hast paid the uttermost farthing." Could He have said this if the prison-doors were never to be thrown open? These words are in agreement with the truth that future punishment is remedial and terminable; they are certainly hostile to the idea that it is hopeless and unending.

In Matt. xii. 32, our Lord's comment upon the sin against the Holy Spirit is—"It shall not be forgiven him, neither in this age ($\alpha\iota\acute{\omega}\nu$); neither in the one to come." That is, Christ declares this particular sin to be so great, that for *two æons* forgiveness will be withheld. But there will be ages, after this present one and the next one shall have passed away. Will there be no forgiveness *then?* His words imply that there will be. When we tell a bad child that he will be punished this week and next week, we do not proclaim that his punishment will never come to an end.

In Luke vi. 27–35, our Lord says,—"Love your enemies; do good to them which hate you; bless them that curse you," etc., etc., and adds, "And ye shall be the children of the Highest: for He is kind unto the unthankful and to the evil. Be ye, therefore, merciful, as your Father also is merciful."

Is this true of God, if future punishment be hopeless and everlasting? In that case, is He kind and merciful to the evil? And are we to act toward our enemies in the implacable and remorseless spirit in which, as some theologians have said, God will act toward His enemies?

In 1 John iii. 8, it is declared that the son of God "was manifested that He *might destroy* the works of the devil."

All are agreed that sin and alienation from God are included in that definition of evil. But if sin be incurable, and alienation perpetual, will this prophecy concerning the Son of God ever be fulfilled? What, therefore, is the conclusion at which we arrive, when we have stripped certain passages of Scripture of the false meaning imported into them by mistranslation, and have considered those many other passages whose magnificent import has been ignored?

This—that the Future Punishment of God will not be what Western Christendom for centuries has declared they will be; but that they will be Fatherly, remedial and terminable.

A difficulty, which presents itself to some, in accepting the foregoing conclusion.

This difficulty is expressed in some such way as follows:

If the Greek word αἰώνιος, when applied to terms which refer to Future Punishment, does not mean " eternal" or "everlasting," but "aionial," or that which pertains to a limitable age, then the same word cannot mean " eternal" or " everlasting" when applied to such terms as " life," " glory," " redemption," and "salvation." Consequently, what guarantee have we that the life, the glory, and salvation bestowed through Christ will be *everlasting?* " You tell me," says the objector, " that the judgments and punishments of God are terminable, because they are described by the word αἰώνιος ; and that word does *not* mean 'everlasting.' Then is not the life and salvation, described by the same word, also terminable?" This, at first sight, appears a very formidable question; but the answer is a very simple one. The word αἰώνιος does not, in regard to either set of passages, denote "everlasting" or "eternal." When our Lord said,—" He believing on the Son hath *aionial* (αἰώνιος) life" (John iii. 36); and "I give unto them *aionial* (αἰώνιος) life " (John x. 28)—He did not promise an *everlasting* life in those words, but the life pertaining to an age, or æon.

The reader will remember that St. Paul, in Eph. iii. 21, speaks of " all the generations of *the æon* of the æons."

Our Lord was referring to this; and the life He promised was " the life of this æon "—*i. e.*, the life characterizing that vast age with all its generations or epochs, during which the great purpose of God will be worked out. He declared that those who accepted Him would be in a condition of life and blessedness all through this aionial period.

In Heb. v. 9, salvation is described as αἰώνιος; *i. e.*, a salvation which is the characteristic "of the ages."

In Heb. ix. 12, redemption, too, is described by the same adjective, because it is a redemption which will be worked out during those ages.

The life given by Christ will continue when "the life of the æon" shall have ended. We shall live on and be blessed, when that vast epoch in which God will have worked out His purpose of sav-

ing mankind shall have melted into the infinite
past.

But the guarantee of our everlastingness is not to
be found in that oft-repeated promise of the Saviour
—to give *aionial* life to His faithful servants.

We should be in a sorry plight had we to base
our hopes of immortality on the meaning of a
Greek word (αἰώνιος), which word has been applied
to the doors of a Temple no longer in existence.

Oh! no; the guarantee that the life imparted by
Christ will be an unending one, and that the glory
that will accrue to us as redeemed souls will be an
everlasting glory, rests upon a far securer basis than
that. It is founded on the fact that man by Christ
is brought into close and vital relationship with
God. Associated with Him, he is associated with
a Being who possesses an *indestructible* life—a
God-life; and this indestructible life is imparted,
and will be imparted, to every member of the
human race as soon as he is, or shall be, united to
Him.

"As in Adam *all* die, even so in Christ shall *all*
be made alive," wrote the Apostle. Yes, and the

" all " who shall be made alive by the living Christ, shall never cease to live, because the eternal Son of God from whom they shall draw their life is the deathless Head of the race.

So, then, not upon the words αἰών and αἰώνιος, so perplexingly and arbitrarily treated by translators, do we ground our hope of immortality, but upon such declarations in the Word of God as these: "Because *I* live, *ye* shall live also" (John xiv. 19); "Your life is hid with Christ in God" (Col. iii. 3); "In Him was life . . . and *of His fulness have we all received*" (John i. 4, 16); "As I live by the Father; so he that eateth Me, even he *shall live by Me*" (John vi. 57); "I am come that they might have life, and *that they might have it above measure*" (John x. 10); "The law of the spirit of life in Christ Jesus hath made me *free from the law of sin and death*" (Rom. viii. 2). And, surely, the eternal fitness of things suggests that the everlastingness of the saved must be, and will be, the grand consummation of the great All-Father's "Purpose of the ages"!

THE END.

CPSIA information can be obtained
at www.ICGtesting.com
Printed in the USA
LVHW080610111218
599931LV00022BA/942/P